Prai

"A powerful and compelling ... is a must read for everyone, especially Millennials who are searching for meaning. This book will change you and your world for the better. I loved it and couldn't put it down. I wish I had read a book like this when I became a lawyer. It would have deepened my faith and brought more meaning to my work."

—**Elizabeth Yore,** international child legal counsel

"This generation is obsessed with social justice, but rarely the kind that comes at any personal cost. Comment sections, Facebook filters, and Snap Chat stories have given the whole world a chance to get angry, but rarely to get involved. Kristi's book—a practical and passionate work of get-off-the-couch journalism—could not have come at a better time. It's the kind of book that makes you rethink why you're here."

—**Brian Ivie,** director of the documentary *The Drop Box*

"It's about time the church took back the term 'justice' from those who have jettisoned the real Gospel in favor of one that elevates the state instead of Christ. Credit to Kristi for doing that, as well as for challenging believers to remember and obey the words of Micah 6:8."

—**Steve Deace,** nationally syndicated radio show host, Salem Radio Network and Conservative Review

"*Do Justice* is for those unwilling to hide behind the isolated walls of the Kingdom's already established territory. It offers hope for those willing to recapture God-void lands and live between the tension of social justice and authentic Gospel. It's a refreshing dose of reality for those bold enough to pray like Solomon for 'discernment in administering justice.'"

—**Gene Roncone,** pastor, Highpoint Church, Aurora, CO

"With passion, conviction, and biblical insight far beyond her years, Kristi Brown describes the plight of various people groups and explains how God's people can meet desperate needs, both physically and spiritually, expanding far beyond the typical things many others suggest. Her heart for the 'least of these' is truly contagious and her wisdom valuable."

—**Glenn T. Stanton,** director for Family Formation Studies at Focus on the Family

"*Do Justice* is a clarion call to Biblical action. In an era of political correctness motivating many to retreat from cultural battle lines, Kristi Burton Brown reminds us that pseudoneutrality in the face of injustice is not Christian duty. Brown not only guides us in revisiting the most pressing moral matters of our day, such as elective abortion, but reminds us of the real human lives at stake. We must not wait on others to act when we see our neighbors in need. Following in the footsteps of our Savior, we must take action now. Indeed, we must *do* justice."

—**Seth Drayer,** director of training at Created Equal

KRISTI BURTON BROWN

DO JUSTICE

PRACTICAL WAYS TO ENGAGE OUR WORLD

DO JUSTICE

Practical Ways to Engage Our World

ISBN 978-089112-461-0

Printed in the United States of America

Library of Congress Cataloging-in-Publication Data is on file at the Library of Congress, Washington, DC.

Cover design by ThinkPen Design, LLC, and Strong Design
Interior text design by Sandy Armstrong, Strong Design

Leafwood Publishers is an imprint of Abilene Christian University Press
ACU Box 29138
Abilene, Texas 79699

1-877-816-4455
www.leafwoodpublishers.com

17 18 19 20 21 22 / 7 6 5 4 3 2 1

Contents

Introduction

When our grandchildren ask us where we were when the voiceless and the vulnerable of our era needed leaders of compassion and purpose, I hope we can say that we showed up, and that we showed up on time.
—Gary Haugen, International Justice Mission president and CEO

Dear Friend,

Imagine you are at your kitchen table with invigorating music flowing through your surround sound system. Tonight you're looking forward to dinner with some friends at a new hip restaurant in town. You have some time, so you're flipping through the web on your phone.

And suddenly, time stands still.

Zooming in front of your face, a video shows you what is happening in real life. You can hear the *clack*, *clack*, *clack* of a train and see a bony arm extending feebly from a cattle car. You can practically smell the thick smoke from the funnel as it billows out. The gnawing *clank* of chains crashes in on you, and then you see them: hundreds of slaves being forced down the lowered plank of a slave ship. There's a house to your right, and through the cracked door you can see young girls huddling on a bed, about to be trafficked for a few dollars.

Your screen goes black and opens to a new scene: a woman lying on a cold operating table with doctors at the ready to extract and terminate a breathing, unborn life. With another flash, you see a dirty, ragged child shivering underneath a streetlight, lacking even a sweat shirt to keep him warm.

These visions of horror and injustice close in on you, each face getting closer and closer to your own. With one voice, they cry out, "Who will do justice for us?"

Each of these scenarios is played out daily, next door to us and a world away. If we could actually *see* these tragedies, this oppression, with our own eyes—if we could hear and smell and feel it—what would we do differently? What would we stop doing? What would we be willing to give up and change?

Would we say that working for justice is the job of the "cause people"? Would we say we weren't made for such things? Would we shrink back in fear instead of lunging forward in faith? Or would we make the choice to live like Christians—to live like followers of the God-Man Who sought justice every day He walked this earth?

I don't claim to have all the solutions to the problems of our day. Instead, my goal in this book is to present various cases for justice and to share the stories of those who have gone before: brave Christians who have taken the issues of the world upon their own shoulders, demonstrating an active, loving, and just Christ to a needy, suffering world. I want to inspire you to do the same.

May both you and I be like our brothers and sisters whose stories fill the pages of this book, always remembering that we are surrounded by a cloud of witnesses urging us on to the finish line. May we start well, run well, and end well. May we work diligently as the good, faithful servants of God, Who has called and equipped us. Nothing we do could ever earn our salvation, but all we do is in honor of the Savior, Who gave all for us. It's been said that God doesn't require us to be good before He loves us; His love is what makes us good.

Our goal should be twofold: first, to bring justice to a world that neglects the needy, treads on the suffering, oppresses the oppressed, and pounds down the weak; and second—and most important—to bring Christ to a world that needs Him above all else. If we bring Christ, we have succeeded, even if the world calls our attempt a failure. Christ is the definition of hope and justice, and when we work where He calls us, there is profound, eternal victory.

While I was writing this book, my husband reminded me that Christ Himself is actively working for justice in our world, even though He knows it won't be ultimately fulfilled until He returns. As Isaiah 42:3–4 says, "In faithfulness he [prophesying about Jesus] will bring forth justice; he will not falter or be discouraged till he establishes justice on earth." Let us not falter or be discouraged. Let us not waver in the midst of our adversity. Our own strength might be limited, but God's strength within us is boundless.

In this book, I will cover many of the issues that are particularly important to our generation. However, there are altogether too many to mention; so many issues cry out for us to do justice. Find the cause that God has put on your heart—whether or not it's covered here—and do justice in your circle of influence. Broaden that circle, or close it in, if need be.

I hope to encourage all of us to pick up our crosses together, to bear each other's burdens, and to be the voices crying out for justice somewhere—whether it's in a prayer closet at home, at a Bible study, on a campus, behind a computer screen, with our children, in our neighborhoods, on a public stage, behind a pulpit, or on a television broadcast that shouts out to the entire world.

My parents taught me that we were created for a much greater purpose than ourselves. We are here for others; we are here for God;

we are here to be the hands and feet of Christ. You have a calling that is all your own. There is a reason you are here on earth at this exact moment in history. There is a vision for you to catch, a journey for you to take, and a mission for you to accomplish.

I pray that you will have a flame lit under your feet that will speed you along in your quest to do justice for the people God lays on your heart. Despite the obstacles in your path, don't turn back. Just go. Simply obey, trusting God all the way. Let Him open the doors, make a path where there is none, and part the sea for you. On the other side of the eternal River Jordan, you will understand the whys, and you will see that your journey was worth it all along.

No matter the weariness, the cost, or the sacrifice, if you obediently follow in the footsteps of Christ as you do justice, you will hear the precious words one day: "Well done, good and faithful servant. Enter now into thy rest" (Matt. 25:21).

Remember that the systems that promote injustice are not too big to take on if we seek the real justice of God. A peaceful revolution and reformation are not out of reach.

CHAPTER ONE

A Maverick for Life

The only thing necessary for evil to prevail is for good men to do nothing.
—Edmund Burke

Until 2006, I was just a small-town, homeschooled country girl. At the age of nineteen, one year after I started law school, I decided to take on the state of Colorado. I believed that God was laying a fight for justice on my heart, and I wanted to participate.

There's an important vision wrapped up in this book that I hope we can all catch:

1. There is *so much* work to do in this world. So many issues cry out for resolution, for the people of God to act, and for the heart of God to be seen.
2. No matter where you are, who you are, or how much or how little you have, you can do something to bring God's justice. In fact, you must.
3. You might fail. You probably will. What matters most is that you try again.

In this book, you'll hear not only my story but the stories of many others. You'll see what they've done for justice, but most important, I hope you'll be inspired for *what you can do*. Together as the body of Christ, we can do justice in a suffering world that cries out for it. Micah 6:8 (ESV) instructs us: "He has told you, O man, what is good; and what does the LORD require of you but to do justice, and to love kindness, and to walk humbly with your God?"

In doing justice, some of us will give our money; some our time. Some of us can work full time on these issues; others part time. Regardless of our differences, the heart of justice is the same, because it is the heart of God. It's not a competition, but it is a race. And in this race, we run with our eyes fixed on Jesus (Heb. 12:1–3).

When we focus on Jesus, our hearts become more like His. He will enable us to do justice without losing our resolve. Remember, He has already overcome sin and death. The grave is nothing for Him, and it is nothing for us.

Out of the many issues of justice, saving the lives of innocent, preborn babies is my personal calling. I fully believe that stopping abortion and making it unthinkable are real and achievable. The pro-life movement is rooted in true compassion for babies *and* their mothers; it's rooted in justice for entire families and equality for women and children.

My Story

At nineteen, I became the cosponsor of a constitutional amendment in Colorado that sought to include every human being in the definition of "person." To me, this seemed like a simple and self-evident concept, but our laws don't actually recognize that every human is a person. And because the unborn are not considered true persons, abortion is allowed at all stages of pregnancy. Tragically, these young lives are terminated—sometimes in violent and horrific fashion.

The 2008 Colorado Personhood Campaign was designed to change all that. State and national news picked up the story, and as a spokesperson, I was interviewed by *The Washington Times*, *Newsweek*, and *U.S. News & World Report*, among others. The first real debate of my life (I'd had plenty of less serious ones with my younger brother) was on live television against a woman who was a seasoned, committed abortion advocate. I was literally shaking in my seat next to her, hoping she couldn't see.

I was called many things during the campaign:

- "A right-wing Christian fundamentalist"[1]
- "Cracker of the week"[2]
- "Face of 'personhood' issue young, resolute"[3]
- "Not exactly beloved by the antiabortion movement"[4]
- "The wind-up doll"[5]
- "A young true believer"[6]
- "Maverick for life"[7]

People sent me e-mails wishing I would be raped or have a miscarriage. They called my parents vulgar names. I was sent a used condom in a greeting card. But a little girl also sent me a beautiful drawing of her and me standing together. Countless people promised to pray and sent in their hard-earned financial support. There was so much beauty amid the ugliness.

One of my most embarrassing and precious moments came when I was interviewed by the Colorado Medical Board. They were deciding whether they would support the Personhood Amendment. Despite a vast amount of medical evidence that clearly demonstrated that human life began at fertilization, the board voted to oppose the amendment.

At the meeting, I felt mocked and ridiculed, but rarely in my life have I felt so peaceful and confident. I knew that I was exactly where I was supposed to be and that God was doing something I couldn't see.

I could tell you much more about the campaign. I could talk about the beauty of seeing God's people come together to sing and pray and save lives. I could talk about what it feels like to silently march along sidewalks with a group of prayer warriors, praying for life. I know what it's like to be told it's wrong for you to lead because you're a woman, that you don't have what it takes, that God is displeased with you, and that someone else is a better choice than you. I know how it feels to have your confidence marred, your dreams crushed, and your faith shaken.

But I also understand how it feels to know that a large section of humanity is behind you and agrees with you—that many, many people are glad to know the truth and that they stand with you in the defense of life. I know how it feels to speak to a crowd of thousands in a sports arena—daring to tell them to vote for a pro-life slate of candidates, defying the powers that be—and to get the seventh-most votes out of dozens of people running. I know how it feels to *realize* that God is with you and that He is making all things new.

One of my favorite stories of the campaign comes from a church in northern Colorado. One Sunday, a man was praying in front of the whole congregation about the Personhood Amendment. He prayed that God would open the eyes of the voters and help them see that these babies are truly people worth saving. That morning, a young woman who had an abortion scheduled for a few days later was in attendance. When she drove to her appointment, the man's prayer came back to her. She called her boyfriend on the spot and told him that she couldn't go through with the abortion; they were keeping the baby.

My mom has always told me, "Your power is in your prayer." God has gifted His people with a special power in prayer. The words of that faithful man's simple prayer were used to open the eyes of a mother so that she could see the beauty and value of her little baby's life. For that family, the whole world was changed on Sunday.

On election night in November 2008, we lost. I have little memory of what I said in my concession speech. I know it wasn't the speech I wanted to give. But this I do know: *God was there.* Always. On every step of my journey. Every time I fell on my face. Every time my hopes were dashed. Every time I thought it was about me. Every time I thought about all the babies I couldn't save. Every time. *He was there.*

The Presence of God

Before you even start thinking about social justice—before you even consider where you should go and what battles you should fight—know this: God will be there with you every step of the way. No matter what others say. No matter if you succeed or fail. No matter if you save lives or if they are lost anyway. No matter if people hate you or love you. God will be there just as He was with Moses, with Esther, with David, with Gideon, with Dorcas, with Deborah, with Peter, with me. He will be with you too. Never forget that.

After losing the campaign, I was asked if we were going to quit. It was a fact then and now that we can never give up. In the grand scheme of things—however personal it was to me—this was just one loss. If you believe in something, you don't quit after one try. Even if one try takes two years, thousands of dollars, thousands of people, and countless hours. Even if your hopes and dreams and millions of lives are wrapped up in it. You try again until you succeed. You try until every single life is saved.

All we see today are the effects of sin and death all around us. That's what injustice is. Yet as Christians, we can have faith that the final victory of biblical justice will always be ours because it's already Christ's. He has already conquered sin and death itself. We have nothing to fear because we know that on the other side of the battle we fight today is life everlasting.

When my faith was renewed after struggling with the loss, I knew that it was more beautiful and precious to me than ever before. I had new eyes to see God; He made more sense to me. And with my renewed faith came a steady determination to see my mission through to the end.

I still firmly believe that I am called to help stop abortion. For now, the avenues have changed, but the passion and the fight are still there. When we work for justice with God, there is no such thing as defeat. We just have to learn how to get up again. As Proverbs 24:16 (NLT) reminds us, "The godly [also translated *just*] may trip seven times, but they will get up again." So we fight. And win or lose, we rise again.

Christian determination means being committed to the end goal, however it looks at various points of our lives and whether one person or thousands listen to us. From the ages of nineteen to twenty-one, I was a political figure. Now, as a young stay-at-home mom, I'm a journalist, editor, policy fellow, and part-time attorney for the pro-life cause. I have a vision for getting more deeply involved on the legal side of abortion one day. But no matter what justice work looks like in my future, I'm determined to let God use me as *He* sees fit.

I love how Sarah Ray, a millennial entrepreneur who helps women escape the bonds of human trafficking and poverty, puts it: "Do something. Do it with Jesus. And don't stop doing it until Jesus moves you on to the next thing. God doesn't choose the most qualified. He chooses those who say *yes*."[8]

I must keep in step with God's calling. He has chosen that His people should live for justice, and that means caring about little things as well as big things. Each one is worthy of my time. It all comes down to listening to His voice and choosing to walk in faithfulness. Do I believe that God has placed His call for justice in my heart? Am I being attentive to His will, realizing that it all comes down to God and me?

CHAPTER TWO

Christians in the Culture

Fear not, little flock, for it is your Father's good pleasure to give you the kingdom.
—LUKE 12:32

Whether we feel called to reach out in our own neighborhood or travel ten thousand miles to make contact with an isolated tribe, there's one premise we can all agree on: *Christians are desperately needed in every culture of the world.*

Instead of debating where the needs are the greatest and what work really produces the "best" results, we should hone in on the issue God has laid on *our* heart and work in faithfulness from there. It's impossible to quantify the greatness of any particular need, the likelihood of success, or the effect of succeeding. There's a reason we aren't all-knowing. Serving God isn't a formula; it's a lifestyle.

A service lifestyle definitely doesn't include competing against other Christians or measuring the effect of their justice work against our own. We can be motivated or challenged by their work, but we shouldn't idolize or denigrate them. While we should tell others about the justice issues God has given us a passion for—and even encourage them to get involved—we should also be respectful and grateful when God uses Christians elsewhere.

No souls are more worth saving than others; our Savior came to save us all. While on earth, He healed physical bodies and saved our souls from hell. We are truly the body of Christ—His hands reaching out across the world, being present in each corner, no matter how small. Regardless of where or who we serve, our focus needs to be on bringing the love, truth, and justice of Christ to the culture we're in. First Peter 4:10–11 reminds us: "As each has received a gift, use it to serve one another, as good stewards of God's varied grace: whoever speaks, as one who speaks oracles of God; whoever serves, as one who serves by the strength that God supplies—in order that in everything God may be glorified through Jesus Christ."

The bottom line is that no Christian's social justice service is more important than another's, as long as we follow our own God-given calling. Let the world hate, let the talking heads spout, and let the waters rage. God is still on His throne, working miracles, and enabling us to accomplish His work throughout the nations. Despite the attempted sidetracking or outright ridicule of those around us, we have one job: to be faithful. We must love our neighbors with the heart of Christ in any culture, *wherever in the world they might be.*

What Is Justice?

The importance of defining terms cannot be overemphasized. I've been asked more than once, "How do you define justice?" Since the premise of this entire book is doing justice, let's confirm what exactly "justice" includes. In a world that cries out for equality, tolerance, nondiscrimination, privacy, and individual rights, do Christians know what true justice is?

While some might be turned off by the term "social justice," there is a biblical basis for real social justice. We just need to know what it is and how to define it as Christians. Whenever we speak out about social justice, it's important to make sure—as one pastor reminded me—that we are all talking about the same thing. Psalm 89:14 says, "Righteousness and justice [or judgment] are the foundation of Your throne; love and faithfulness go before You." Love and action, it would seem, flow from God's throne of justice and righteousness. Therefore, justice is all about action: finding solutions, strategizing, organizing, speaking out, and mobilizing. It is the very essence of "doing." In addition, justice has a few constant companions: righteousness, faithfulness, mercy, and truth. We need to look upon a needy and suffering world with the goal of taking the reformation and revolution of justice upon ourselves.

We discover what is right in the eyes of God through two simple, and yet sometimes complex, ways. First, we read, study, and devour His Word. Second, we seek His face through prayer and worship, through constant communion with the Almighty. He spoke through His inspired, inerrant Word—as "holy men of God" were "carried along by the Holy Spirit" (2 Pet. 1:21)—and He speaks through that same Word today.

He also places burdens and passions in our hearts. He gives words to our lips. He provides direction to our steps. And yet God will not tell us to do or to say anything that contradicts His Word. If it contradicts Scripture, it is not of God.

Pastor Gene Roncone provides an excellent perspective on social justice for Christians: "Social justice absent of the gospel is empty. I love the passion for social justice that millennials have. I do get concerned that some of them do justice at the expense of evangelism. Compassion absent of life transformation is toxic."[1]

If we study Scripture, we know that biblical justice includes a number of things—some that we have yet to thoroughly examine. Millennial Christian leader Seth Silvers puts it this way: "Justice looks like those who are being oppressed having a voice to speak up and those doing the oppression being held responsible for their acts. The definition of justice does not change from person to person. Justice looks like lives being valued, life being promoted, and people living in a world where they have the opportunity and capability to grow and develop into the people they were created to be."[2]

Justice is often furthered by generosity. Throughout the Bible, we see God's followers reject the idea that their possessions belong to them alone. Instead, they have the view that their days, time, money, and possessions all belong to God, to be used for His higher purposes. One pastor writes that true, biblical justice "reflects the character of God" because "He identifies with the powerless. He takes up their cause."

Taking up the cause of the powerless involves doing difficult things. We might be called to act boldly, to speak with courage, and to go against the majority of society. Oftentimes, "justice" is not as acceptable as "compassion." But as Reggie Littlejohn shares, "I've noticed that people in general are more comfortable participating in mercy ministries—feeding the homeless, visiting the sick, visiting those who are in prison. It's really hard to get people behind a justice cause . . . and I wonder if that's because people are more comfortable expressing compassion as opposed to expressing opposition or being courageous in standing up against something, because when you're dealing with a justice issue, you are standing up for someone, and you are also standing against oppressive forces that are harming them."[3]

Pastor Robert Gelinas had this to say about social justice: "I just think [true social justice issues] are all gospel issues. The gospel addresses personal transformation and salvation, and the gospel addresses societal transformation and salvation, and so I would just say, let it be part of your faith. It *is* part of our faith. Let it be normal."[4]

We could do more justice if we accepted it as a basic biblical issue and a normal part of our Christian walk. Jesus illustrates both the necessity and the normalcy of doing justice. While He is ever merciful and compassionate, He is equally just. As many have observed, Jesus chose people rejected by society, He challenged inequitable cultural norms, He fearlessly but respectfully faced off with those in power when necessary, and He raised His voice to aid the oppressed.

When Jesus returns, He will rule as the powerful king Who brings justice to this broken earth (Acts 17:31). Christ-followers should long for the coming of our Lord. He has blessings in store for those who faithfully walk with Him in justice and righteousness during their earthly lives:

> These will wage war against the Lamb, and the Lamb will overcome them, because He is Lord of lords and King of kings, and those who are with Him are the called and chosen and faithful. (Rev. 17:14)

> Now there is in store for me the crown of righteousness, which the Lord, the righteous Judge, will award to me on that day—and not only to me, but also to all who have longed for his appearing. (2 Tim. 4:8)

When we fear or waver in our fight to do justice, we can remember that one day—one glorious day—the true reformer Who can do all justice will come:

> Say to Daughter Zion, "See, your Savior comes!" (Isa. 62:11)

> Fear not, daughter of Zion; behold, your king is coming! (John 12:15)

As one pastor says, the "call to justice [is] inescapable." The "how," or the application—well, that's between you and God.

Quin Friberg, a millennial Christian leader, reminds us that front and center in our fight for justice is the gospel of Christ. The deepest need of any human being is a personal, saving relationship with Jesus Christ:

> We need to step back and look at the big picture once in a while. We need to remember our ultimate goal as followers of Christ is not to make this world perfect, but to lead people to Christ so they can spend eternity with Him in the life to come. There is a saying that if you give a starving man food and send him on his way, you're just sending him off to an eternity separated from God with a full stomach. I really do look at it that way: This is all temporary, and this will all pass away. If I do not have an eternal perspective when dealing with social justice issues, there isn't much point in dealing with them.[5]

Cultural Christians in the Bible

Many millennials wonder about the relevance of some biblical issues in contemporary culture. And while Christians should evaluate the words we use and the way we communicate, we don't want to become just like the culture around us.

The first, middle, and last thing we want to do is become more like Jesus. As Bethany Hoang from International Justice Mission says, "Seeking justice begins with seeking God: our God who longs to bring justice; our God who longs to use *us*, every one of his children, to bring justice; our God who offers us the yoke of Jesus in exchange for the things that otherwise leave us defeated."[6] As we seek Him, He will teach us that His peace comes when we pursue justice, that He is the God of compassion and righteousness and justice, and that we need to follow in His footsteps in all these areas. And He will teach us more than we could ever learn on our own.

Immersing ourselves too deeply in cultural lifestyles is like immersing the proverbial frog in a pot of gradually heating water. As we grow accustomed to the surrounding social environment, the sin doesn't seem so bad to us. We don't see a reason to speak up. Before we know it, we're so accepting of the sin, we're now the ones participating in it. We begin to think it's OK to pray for permission to commit sins that the Bible clearly tells us to refrain from. Eventually we think we hear God telling us that these sins aren't actually sins anymore. Unfortunately, this is where looking for relevance often leads us.

When Jesus prayed for His people—for *us*—He made it clear that while we have purposely been put in this world by God, we are not of this world. Our goal is not to be accepted by the world but to introduce the world to the Savior:

> I have given them Your word and the world has hated them, for they are not of the world any more than I am of the world. My prayer is not that You take them out of the world but that You protect them from the evil one. They are not of the world, even as I am not of it. Sanctify them by the truth; Your word is truth. As You sent Me into the world, I have sent them into the world. . . . My prayer is not for them alone. I pray also for those who will believe in Me through their message. . . . Then the world will know that You sent me and have loved them even as you have loved Me. (John 17:14–23)

Christian lives should be modeled after the life of Jesus. He reached out to sinners, but He never participated in their sin. Jesus was so obedient to God's commands, Philippians 2:8 tells us that He was "obedient to death." Since when have we had to risk death by being obedient? And yet, this is the standard of obedience and difference from the world that followers of Christ are called to. Let's take, as examples, the lives of Elijah, Paul, Jeremiah, and Solomon.

Elijah: The Bold Prophet Who Hid

Elijah is almost a study in contradictions. One day, he would boldly call out the false prophets of Baal, and the next day, he would run and hide in a cave, lamenting that there was no one else like him in all the land who still worshipped the one true God.

Of course, God knew just how to deal with Elijah. He told Elijah the truth: many others had still not bowed their heads to Baal. God comforted Elijah with His still, small voice, and He provided him a place of respite with the widow of Zarephath. Eventually God called Elijah back to be a bold voice in a nation that was turning away from God.

Clearly, Elijah felt like he was different from his culture. And in many ways—perhaps the most obvious ones—he was. But Elijah determined that he was *God's* servant, not a servant of this world. Even when he thought that the king might kill him, he did not assimilate into the sinful culture of his day. Elijah remained a bold witness, and he is one of only two men in Scripture who did not die but were taken up to heaven.

Paul: The Apostle of Suffering

Paul describes how he was treated by the people of his day in 2 Corinthians 11:23–28:

> I have . . . been exposed to death again and again. Five times I received from the Jews the forty lashes minus one. Three times I was beaten with rods, once I was pelted with stones, three times I was shipwrecked, I spent a night and a day in the open sea, I have been

> constantly on the move. I have been in danger from rivers, in danger from bandits, in danger from my fellow Jews, in danger from Gentiles; in danger in the city, in danger in the country, in danger at sea; and in danger from false believers. I have labored and toiled and have often gone without sleep; I have known hunger and thirst and have often gone without food; I have been cold and naked. Besides everything else, I face daily the pressure of my concern for all the churches.

Sounds like a culturally uncomfortable life, right? Even after all this, Paul was willing to expose himself to ridicule and outsider treatment again, and again, and *again*—all for the cause of Christ. Instead of being a part of the culture, Paul was determined to change it. I think it would be fair to say that the first famous Christian missionary was successful in his quest.

Jeremiah: The Man Who Would Not Be Silent

A man of woes. A man of extreme calling. Jeremiah was persecuted by his own people, and God told him not to marry or have children, but he was also called in his youth—chosen in his mother's womb—to speak of justice in his culture. He spoke this justice with a heart of compassion, and just like Christ, he wept over Jerusalem.

In Jeremiah 5, God asked Jeremiah to go through Jerusalem to find even one man who "does justice and seeks truth" so that the city could be pardoned. Jeremiah lived a life of speaking aloud, despite great persecution and hatred. He was exiled to a foreign country; he was beaten severely; he was nearly killed more than once; he was thrown into a cistern, where it took thirty men to rescue him; he was placed in stocks; he suffered mentally and physically again and again. His family, hometown, and religious peers and leaders all rejected him.

Some say that "in matters of pain and persecution, Jeremiah the prophet may be considered the Paul of the Old Testament. Perhaps no other pre-Calvary prophet suffered as much for God as did Jeremiah."[7] Needless to say, Jeremiah's culture did not approve of him. And yet, no matter the personal cost, Jeremiah *would not be silent.*

Solomon: The King Who Requested Justice

While it is popularly believed that Solomon asked God for wisdom, what he actually requested was much more profound. He asked God for the ability to do justice—something that naturally requires wisdom. Notice these words from Solomon's prayer in 1 Kings 3: "Give your servant a discerning heart to govern your people and to distinguish between right and wrong. For who is able to govern this great people of yours?"

God was pleased that Solomon had asked for wisdom, and as a result, God offered him this blessing: "Since you have asked for this and not for long life or wealth for yourself, nor have asked for the death of your enemies but for discernment in administering justice, I will do what you have asked" (1 Kings 3:9–12).

Just like Solomon, the wisest human king, let us ask God for this blessing. Let us ask for God's "discernment in administering justice" in our spheres of influence; we don't have to be a king or queen to do justice and impact our culture.

Cultural Christians through the Centuries—and Today

Christians are the people of reform, and it's been that way throughout history. As we do justice, the world needs to look into our lives and see Christ. If Christ cannot be easily discerned in our daily lives and in our justice work, we need to stop and examine ourselves. How do we pass our time, use our words, spend our money, share our social media posts? Are we conformed to the world or transformed by the power of Christ?

As we live and work in our culture—while refusing to become just like it—we will do justice in a variety of ways. Our callings are unique because, as the body of Christ, we will present Him to the world *together*, each in our own assigned ways. No one of us is better than another of us. The giver is not less than the servant; the servant is not less than the preacher. In the eyes of a just God, we are all equal, chosen, and very loved.

Gladys Aylward, a twentieth-century Christian missionary in China, didn't limit her work to evangelism, though she kept that at the forefront of all she did. Gladys also worked to end the foot-binding of young girls and risked her life to rescue orphans and to promote justice in Chinese prisons.[8]

William Carey, who later became known as the father of modern missions, latched onto a culturally unpopular idea: missions. He was once instructed to curb his enthusiasm and told that God did not need help to "convert the heathen." Yet William pursued the calling to ultimate justice he had received from God, and his life—filled with tragedy and apparent failure—awakened the church in a mighty way. William once wrote, "This indeed is the Valley of the shadow of death for me . . . Oh what would I give for a sympathetic friend to whom I might open my heart. But God is here, who not only has compassion, but is able to save to the uttermost."[9]

Mary Slessor experienced a difficult childhood, and as an adult, she had her abilities and calling from God questioned simply because of her gender. And yet Mary chose to reject fear and cultural ideas that didn't match up with God's view of her as His chosen daughter. She went to Africa in 1875 to speak of Jesus, educate children, provide medical help, and care for unwanted children. In large part, it was thanks to Mary that "twin-murder" was stopped in the tribe she visited. She gained unusual respect for a woman in her time because she chose to trust the Lord instead of conceding to the cultural norms of her day.[10]

The bravery required of justice work, whether we stay close to our homes or travel farther than we've ever dreamed, is foreign to our human hearts but dear to the heart of God. While we know about Gladys Aylward, William Carey, and Mary Slessor, there are many justice doers today whose names we've never heard. Their work hasn't made them into church leaders or applauded public figures, and yet, they are quietly but surely advocating for justice in ways that mirror the heart of God.

Let me introduce you to Jodi Visser. Tall, with beautiful dark hair and expressive eyes, Jodi easily engages crowds of people. She's good at asking questions, but she also has well-formed thoughts of her own to share. One of Jodi's main passions is social justice work. She's traveled internationally, but she can often be found doing work here at home as well.

Jodi has a broad vision for serving people throughout the world, including the "poorest of the poor." She takes the great needs and the suffering of this dying world to heart and supports a number of causes, including medical missions, crisis pregnancy centers, job development, clean water initiatives, child services, and education. Jodi realized that at a basic level, these great causes need money to succeed, so she's chosen to give her own money and help fundraise so that others can be encouraged to give.

For inspiration, Jodi turns to Scripture. Two of her favorite passages are James 1:27 and Matthew 25:31–40. As Jodi has learned, Christ can be found in every corner of the world. He is not hard to find; He is there in the tears of love-starved orphans, in the protruding bellies of those stricken by famine, on the deathbeds of AIDS-infected mothers, in tortured prison cells, and in the freshly scrubbed hands of a child who clutches a cup of clean water for the first time.

Both simple and complicated, human need pierces through different circumstances. It demonstrates that each human being was created by the same God:

> The main needs I see are for truth and the love found in truth. . . . They want purpose and they want hope, and this can only come through a redemptive God in this fallen world.
>
> Justice for all people would be freedom from oppressors of all kinds, including freedom from all the lies they have been told. All will be free when they have put into practice the worship and obedience of an almighty Creator Who is the only one Who has the power to heal all wounds of the past.[11]

This determined woman understands that true justice can only come through a relationship with God, Who created justice:

> I would advise reading Scripture daily and . . . doing your best to live out Jesus's commands in love and daily prayer, always with thanksgiving and supplication. I cannot suggest to someone any specifics on how to seek justice without them knowing Who true justice comes from.
>
> Seeking justice is a spiritual battle, and you must be in the Word of God to be able to fight it [evil]. When you trust and obey, God will do His justice through you, and you will be amazed, and you will see more freedom and more justice than you thought was possible. You will see miracles.

> If ever you feel discouraged, remember, the God of love has already overcome the world; you are His disciple to teach what you know. (see John 16:33)[12]

While few of us will fight for justice in identical ways, as redeemed children, we can spread the peace, love, and truth of God in the unique avenues He gives us. Some, like Jodi Visser, can give materially so justice can be done. Others can open their homes and welcome the needy. Still others can travel the world, meeting the needy in their own shacks, field hospitals, and dying places to bring Christ to them.

Together as the body of Christ, we must demonstrate love through justice to each human being—each a unique and equal creation of the Father in heaven Who loves them. In the midst of all this justice-spreading, let us never forget to keep the gospel front and center. Greg Stier, founder of Dare 2 Share, discussed the "anemic theology that says we are to just preach the gospel with our lives."[13] He continued:

> To counteract this, we just need to read the Gospels and the book of Acts. Jesus and his disciples preached the good news with their lives and their lips. Like the two wings of a plane, both are necessary.
>
> See the whole person. Don't just see the physical needs. When Jesus saw the crowds in Matthew 9:36, "He had compassion on them, for they were harassed and helpless, like sheep without a shepherd." He saw past just their physical needs into their shattered and torn souls and offered them hope. If [we] can gain a perspective like Jesus, [we] can follow in His pattern to heal the hurting both physically and spiritually.
>
> If we don't seek to introduce those whom we are serving to Jesus, we are doing them a great injustice.

After all, if we had the cure to cancer and those we were feeding had cancer, wouldn't we feed them *and* give them the cure? Of course we would! Well, we have the cure to something infinitely worse than cancer, and those who die without Jesus are headed somewhere infinitely worse than death. It would be a grave injustice to not share "the cure" with them. The cure is the gospel of Jesus Christ.[14]

CHAPTER THREE

Abortion

The Voices Who Cannot Speak for Themselves

Our lives begin to end the day we become silent about the things that matter.
—Martin Luther King Jr.

You may choose to look the other way, but you can never say again that you did not know.
—William Wilberforce

Abortion is a pivotal social issue for our generation, but to many in the United States—and sadly, even in the church—the word *abortion* has become merely a medical word, largely devoid of meaning. To bring justice to this issue, Christians need to realize exactly what abortion is. (http://www.abortionprocedures.com is one of the best sources of information about abortion.)

Understandably, the facts might make us cringe. The details of what the Nazis did during the Holocaust, what the KKK did to African Americans, and what occurred during the Khmer Rouge genocide in Cambodia are horrific, to say the least. However, cold, hard statistics often inspire people to act.

By September 2, 1945, approximately six million Jews and five million non-Jews had been massacred by the Nazi regime. We call this the Holocaust. By the end of July 1994, an estimated five hundred thousand to one million Rwandans were killed in their own country.[1] We call this genocide. By the end of 2014, more than fifty-seven million babies had been aborted in the United States.[2] Worldwide, that number—counting from 1980—has reached approximately 1,325,622,000.[3] What do we call this? As former president of South Africa Nelson Mandela said, "There can be no keener revelation of a society's soul than the way in which it treats its children."[4]

Preborn Life: What Does Scripture Say?

Pro-life and women's activist Christina Marie Bennett explains why Christians should view abortion as a biblical justice issue:

> Jesus said He came so we would have life and have it in abundance. All throughout the Scriptures, we see that God is the author of life. In the Judeo-Christian faith, Yahweh [God] is both the creator and the sustainer of life. In the Psalms, we see proclamations that God has knit human beings together in their mother's womb. We see the psalmist in Psalm 139 declare humanity is "fearfully and wonderfully made."
>
> We also see in the Old Testament verses that God hates the shedding of innocent blood. One of the seven things listed in Proverbs 6 that God hates is "hands that shed innocent blood." In biblical times, the Israelites used to sacrifice their sons and daughters to idols to gain prosperity. This practice of killing their children for financial gain angered God.
>
> Although Jesus never specifically mentions the word *abortion*, we can see throughout the Scriptures that God values life, loves children before they are born, and hates

> the shedding of innocent blood. Proverbs 31 challenges believers to be a voice for the voiceless and those who are appointed to die. Proverbs 24 calls for us to rescue those being led away to death.
>
> Children are a dream of God's heart. I myself was rescued from abortion through a miracle of God. As my mom sat in the hospital awaiting her abortion, a janitor told her God would give her the strength to have me. I believe that God adores every child and fights for them to live. To be a follower of Christ is to love children and to fight for their protection.[5]

Most Christians are probably familiar with the verses that tell us that God knows us before we are born (Ps. 139:13–17; Jer. 1:5). We also have the scriptural account of John the Baptist recognizing his Savior when they were both in the wombs of their respective mothers (Luke 1:41). It's not debatable that Scripture recognizes the preborn child as a living human being who is known, valuable, called, and spiritually cognizant.

The Beginning of Life: What Does Science Say?

There is definitive scientific evidence that documents when a new, unique, living human being comes into existence. In a civil society, we should not be free to take the lives of innocent people. One person's right to liberty or privacy should never supersede another person's right to life.

The Declaration of Independence recognized that "all men are *created* equal," not that they were *born* equal. While some people insist that a human being must reach a certain point of mental or physical development before he or she is a person, it is imperative that every single human being is considered a person for the sake of basic rights. The scientific community abounds with evidence that human life begins at the moment of conception.[6] Consider these quotes from scientific textbooks:

> The development of a human being begins with fertilization.[7]
>
> Embryonic life commences with fertilization.[8]
>
> Zygote. This cell, formed by the union of an ovum and a sperm . . . represents the beginning of a human being. The common expression "fertilized ovum" refers to the zygote.[9]

Dr. Jérôme Lejeune, the man who discovered the cause of Down syndrome, had this to say about the reality of valuable human life in the womb:

> Life has a very long history, but each of us has a very definite beginning—the moment of conception . . . A month after conception, a human being is one-sixth of an inch long. The tiny heart has already been beating for a week, and the arms, legs, head and brain have already begun to take shape. At two months, the child would fit into a walnut shell: Curled up, she measures a little more than an inch long. Inside your closed fist, she would be invisible, and you could crush her without meaning to—even without noticing. But if you open your hand, she is virtually complete, with hands, feet, head, internal organs, brain, everything in place. All she needs to do is grow. Look even more closely with a standard microscope, and you'll be able to make out her fingerprints. Everything needed to establish her identity is already in place.[10]

In 2008, the Eighth Circuit Court of Appeals agreed with the findings of the South Dakota Task Force to Study Abortion[11] and quoted Dr. Marie Peeters-Ney, a geneticist and physician, in its ruling:

> "Becoming a member of our species is conferred immediately upon conception. At the moment of conception a human being with 46 chromosomes comes into existence. These chromosomes, the organization, the chromosomal pattern is specifically human. The RNA, the messenger protein, the proteins are distinctly human proteins. So this new human being is a member of our species, and humanity is not acquired sometime along the path, it occurs right at conception." (Senate State Affairs Comm. Hearing at 25.) Dr. Peeters-Ney also stated that an embryo or fetus is whole in the sense that "[a]ll the genetic information sufficient and necessary to mature, and the information that is needed for this human being's entire life is present at the time of conception"; that it is "separate from the mother" because "[t]he genetic program is totally complete and this human being will mature according to his or her own program"; and that it is unique because it has "a totally unique genetic code."[12]

One of the best ways to learn about fetal development—and to visually experience it—is to visit the Endowment for Human Development's (EHD) website (http://www.ehd.org). This scientific research organization has worked with *National Geographic* to produce a stunning DVD portraying life in the womb. Beautiful photos, short videos, and detailed facts are freely available on EHD's site. It's well worth a few minutes to get this priceless education in human life. Here are a few of the incredible details from the EHD about development in the womb in the first trimester—the time period when most abortions occur in the United States:

- At sixteen days, the brain is the first organ to appear—before many women even know they're pregnant.
- At twenty-two days, the heart begins to beat. (Breakthrough scientific research indicates the heart might beat at only sixteen days.)[13]
- The complexity achieved by the embryo in just the first three weeks of development is incredible. . . . Early red blood cell precursors are present in the yolk sac just three weeks after fertilization. . . . Also by three weeks, early blood vessels form throughout the embryo as the network of the early circulatory system begins to take shape.
- A six weeks and two days, there are readable brain waves.
- At six and a half weeks, the baby can move his or her hands. (EHD has videotaped an eight-week-old baby waving.)
- At eight weeks, the brain is highly complex and constitutes almost half of the embryo's total body weight. Growth continues at an extraordinary rate.
- Eight weeks marks the end of the embryonic period. . . . The embryo now possesses more than 90 percent of the structures found in adults.
- At nine weeks, the baby can suck his or her thumb, stretch, and respond to touch.

Abortion: Why "Personally Pro-Life" Isn't Good Enough

A major problem among U.S. Christians and millennials is the belief that being "personally pro-life" is enough. "As long as *I* wouldn't get an abortion," the logic goes, "that's all that matters." Similarly, others argue, "I can't force my beliefs on another woman." Or, "I'm a man; I can't identify with a woman's experience."

However, we would never apply this logic to other issues that threaten human beings:

- *Rape:* As long as *I* wouldn't rape a woman, that's all that matters. No need to make it illegal.
- *Trafficking:* I can't "force" my position on others. Those are *my* beliefs, not necessarily theirs.
- *Murder:* I'm not a mother; I can't identify with the experience of that woman who just drowned her two sons.

And yet, for some reason, we think these arguments are acceptable when it comes to abortion. Are we OK with "personally" opposing the KKK but refusing to actively speak against them? Would we be OK with "personally" abstaining from genocide but standing by while human beings are tortured, abused, and killed? Is that really the kind of person—the kind of Christian—we want to be?

Abortion is a moral evil. It's the legal genocide of our day. But just like with other moral evils that exist around the world, civilized Christians must go beyond the "personal" level and act to stop this injustice. It's not enough to "personally" oppose the unjust and inhumane treatment of another human being, especially when the human being is innocent and helpless. We have to do more.

Abortion: The Role of Planned Parenthood

When questioned about Planned Parenthood, 48 percent of college students did not know that Planned Parenthood performs abortions. In fact, many Americans believe that Planned Parenthood is a health center for women. In reality, it is the top abortion-advancement group in the nation. The facts about Planned Parenthood are clear:

- Planned Parenthood's own annual report admitted that its doctors and nurses perform thirty-seven abortions *every hour*.
- $1.4 million (yes, *million*) is given to Planned Parenthood *every single day* in taxpayer funds. That means you and I are personally being forced to fund them.
- By very conservative estimates, abortion provided $170 million for Planned Parenthood—a full 55.7 percent of its nongovernment clinic income—in 2012. This is despite the claim that abortion is only 3 percent of its services.[14]
- While Planned Parenthood claims to offer options for women, it often turns them away if they desire prenatal care instead of an abortion (providing them with only a referral). A close friend of mine was told by Planned Parenthood that they couldn't help her unless she wanted an abortion. Her referral was to a disconnected number for an OB-GYN.
- Investigations (that you can read firsthand at http://www.liveaction.org) have shown a darker side of Planned Parenthood. There have been reports of the organization accepting donations to abort African American babies, working with a pimp to get abortions for his trafficked girls so they can continue to work on the street, misleading women about the dangers of abortion and the facts of fetal development, and assuring women that their babies will not be kept alive even if they survive an abortion.

The facts about Planned Parenthood and abortion, in all their horror, need to be brought to light so that taxpayers can assess how funding is being used and abused—so Planned Parenthood can be exposed.[15]

Real-Life Justice Role Models

Let's meet a few men and women who have dedicated their lives to doing justice in this area.

A Girl on Fire: Lila Rose and Live Action

When she was nine years old, Lila Rose came across a photo in a book that depicted a tiny baby, bloody and in pieces, thanks to the cruel work of abortion. A determined passion rose up in Lila's heart to save the babies, and the young girl grew into a young woman who would shake up her nation.

In her teenage years, Lila founded Live Action, an organization that continues to oversee undercover investigations into Planned Parenthood and other abortion clinics. Live Action has found evidence of abortion clinics directly lying to women about fetal development and the dangers of abortion. Investigators discovered that some clinics were willing to work with a pimp who trafficked women, accept donations targeting African Americans for abortion, and perform an abortion simply because the baby was a girl.

Lila continues to spearhead the work of Live Action—which has also branched into Live Action News & Opinion—and has garnered the support of youth and millennials across the nation. More than one million Facebook followers receive daily updates about abortion and pro-life work around the world.

One of Lila's inspirations is Sophie Scholl. During World War II, Sophie, along with her brother and a friend, started the White Rose Society on their college campus. They were determined to spread the truth about the Nazi regime. Despite the danger she put herself in, Sophie was certain that speaking the truth about the great injustice of her day was well worth it. She was eventually caught and beheaded. Lila pointed to a quote by Sophie that illustrates the devotion she feels she shares with the late heroine:

> The real damage is done by those millions who want to "survive." The honest men who just want to be left in peace. Those who don't want their little lives disturbed by anything bigger than themselves. Those with no sides and no causes. Those who won't take measure of their own strength, for fear of antagonizing their own weakness. Those who don't like to make waves—or enemies. Those for whom freedom, honour, truth, and principles are only literature. Those who live small . . . die small. It's the reductionist approach to life: if you keep it small, you'll keep it under control. If you don't make any noise, the bogeyman won't find you. But it's all an illusion, because they die too, those people who roll up their spirits into tiny little balls so as to be safe. Safe?! From what? Life is always on the edge of death; narrow streets lead to the same place as wide avenues, and a little candle burns itself out just like a flaming torch does. I choose my own way to burn.[16]

Sophie declared, "Somebody, after all, had to make a start." And this is exactly what Lila Rose is doing in her own nation. Lila has been working to rescue and protect the preborn for more than a decade, and she's showing no signs of slowing down:

> The fact that the crisis remains each day and because it remains—it's actually intensifying—is a huge source of inspiration to fight even more and to fight smarter. Seeing the victories along the way are, of course, also inspiring. Every time we have a report of a life being saved, it's worth every ounce of every struggle, because a life is worth everything. As a Christian, and wanting to do my little part to try to stumble after Christ . . . He laid down His life for each life, and that example means that

> we're meant to lay down our lives for even one life—especially for one life. Of course, we're also called to be ambitious, and that's why we're fighting for the protection of every child. And we're not going to stop until we see that mission accomplished.[17]

Lila believes that because Christians are "called to love the least of these," we are called to protect the preborn children who are targeted for death in our nation:

> We're called to do it in a radical way because Jesus Himself takes on a radical solidarity with the least of these. He says whatever you do for the least of these, you do it for Me, and whatever you *don't* do for the least of these, you *don't* do it for Me. How we treat those who are the weakest and most defenseless is really how we treat Jesus. That's a very challenging teaching. When you take the time to think about it, it requires that we focus our attention on the most desperate people groups. In our country, it's the preborn children who are denied every legal protection, who are denied their most fundamental human rights. And they're denied it by the people who are closest to them, who should protect them and cherish them the most—their parents.[18]

According to Lila, Christians need to view abortion as a whole family issue so that everyone involved can have their true needs met. She explained that the situation can be even more complex, because sometimes "the parents or the mother herself may be in a crisis—an unexpected pregnancy situation." She continues, "The mother may be a victim as a result of pressures she may be experiencing or even an abuse situation. It compounds the crisis, and it makes us even more responsible to rise to the occasion. All of this is crystal clear for the church . . . if we truly care about social justice, we would be rushing to the defense of the weakest."[19]

Lila shares her thoughts on how Christians can and should do justice for the weakest among us, each in our own roles:

> The foundation for everyone is first to recognize the problem and to come to an understanding of it . . . finding out the facts about how severe the problem of abortion is. . . . We need to be aware of the crisis that's affecting our neighbors—the people that are literally down the street from us. The abortion facility literally may be within a mile radius of our own churches. . . .
>
> And then we need to seek God for how we are supposed to respond. It could be through a full-time church ministry, addressing the problem of abortion in our community both proactively and reactively. If there is an issue with a mother who is scared and alone, we offer nonjudgmental support for her at the church. If there are young people who are not being educated, a church can be focused on educating them about these issues, and also about sexual integrity.
>
> Then there's other ways to get involved—whether it's through community organizations, through praying outside the abortion clinic, counseling and getting involved in the community pregnancy center, getting involved politically. We are called to not sit back while secularism runs our country or while relativism—which completely rejects the idea of absolute human rights—runs our country. We're called to lead.[20]

The Nurse Who Held the Truth in Her Hands: Jill Stanek

It took forty-five minutes to change Jill Stanek's life forever. She was a registered nurse, working in labor and delivery, when she was confronted with a baby who survived an abortion. As Jill discovered, it was not at all uncommon for babies to survive abortions in the second and third trimesters and be left to die—sometimes in trashcans:

> One night, a nursing co-worker was taking an aborted Down's syndrome baby who was born alive to our Soiled Utility Room because his parents did not want to hold him, and she did not have time to hold him. I could not bear the thought of this suffering child dying alone . . . in a Soiled Utility Room, so I cradled and rocked him for the 45 minutes that he lived. He was 21 to 22 weeks old, weighed about 1/2 pound, and was about 10 inches long. He was too weak to move very much, expending any energy he had trying to breathe. Toward the end he was so quiet that I couldn't tell if he was still alive unless I held him up to the light to see if his heart was still beating through his chest wall. After he was pronounced dead, we folded his little arms across his chest, wrapped him in a tiny shroud, and carried him to the hospital morgue where all of our dead patients are taken.[21]

Thanks to the work of many, including Jill (who was eventually fired by her hospital for speaking out against its practices), Infant Born Alive protection acts were passed around the nation. These laws dictate that babies who survive abortions cannot be left to die. Sadly, a number of states have still failed to pass these acts, and abortion clinics have been found killing these babies. A Planned Parenthood spokeswoman stated that what happened to babies who survive abortions should be between the mother and her doctor.[22]

Nevertheless, Jill hasn't stopped working to defend innocent life. She is inspired to keep fighting by that little baby she rocked until he died. When she thinks of him and "the overwhelming number of children who are killed by abortion," she remembers why she chose to move from being personally pro-life to actively pro-life. Jill has seen abortion destroy children, families, and cultures, and she is compelled to act by the "overwhelming loss to abortion worldwide."

Through her work, Jill created one of the most popular pro-life blogs in the nation, testified before Congress, and received recognition as one of the nation's thirty most prominent pro-life leaders and one of the ten most feared enemies of the pro-abortion left. In 2015, she accepted a position with the Susan B. Anthony List.

Jill explains why she considers abortion a social justice issue for Christians in particular:

> I don't think you can find a social justice issue that impacts more people. We know that one billion people have been killed worldwide—just in the past two decades—from abortion. That's one-seventh of our population. You can't name another social justice issue or plague or war or earthquake or tsunami that could possibly match the toll that abortion has taken. And it's purposeful; it's not accidental.
>
> Christians know that we are created in the image of God, and when you're looking at innocent human beings, there is no more innocent human being than a preborn child. . . .
>
> The Bible constantly challenges us to care for orphans and widows. Children who are marked for abortion are orphans in the ideological sense. And often their mothers are widows. Oftentimes, their mothers feel forced into abortion because they've been abandoned by their partners. So social justice-wise, on both

> fronts, I think we're called to care for these two people groups—the orphans and their moms.[23]

Jill believes that the church needs to be actively, passionately involved in the abortion issue. She suggested a multitude of ways for churches to do justice—some of them preventative in nature:

> The wrong of abortion should be taught from the pulpit. Just as some pastors clearly preach against porn, we need pastors to just as clearly preach against abortion.
>
> Churches should also be actively involved in trying to stop abortion in their community. If there's an abortion clinic in their community—or they can try to find the nearest one—actively go and pray in front of that abortion clinic and try to persuade moms from abortion; help them.
>
> Education on abortion in the church needs to start young, and it also needs to start with teaching on chastity—the importance of remaining chaste until you're married, that's been lost. And getting married, that's all been lost. Churches also really need to more closely monitor the kids that go to college because that's when we seem to just lose so many. We need to make sure we don't lose them, because that's also the age when the most abortions are committed.

Jill suggests that churches take on a crisis pregnancy center as a ministry. If there is no center in the area, she encourages starting one "because there is a need for that everywhere." Crisis pregnancy centers provide practical help, real options, and facts about abortion and fetal development to men and women. People at these centers can kindly guide women through any difficult circumstances they might face, and they offer healing and recovery programs for those who have already gone through an abortion.

As a mother of three and a grandmother of nine, Jill has seen that millennials have a particular power:

> My experience with millennials is that they're very smart and wise in a different way. They are abortion survivors—even if their mothers are the most pro-life women in the world, they still are a choice, and they still know what it's like. Many of them have lost siblings and appreciate that between one-fourth and one-third of their generation has been killed by abortion. I think they're seeing the devastation that the generation before them has wrought—the free love generation from the sixties that is now in charge of things. . . .
>
> I hope that millennials would not necessarily think of themselves as the future of the pro-life movement, because they're not. They *are* the pro-life movement. They're incredibly vital, and the other side just fears them. The other side doesn't have millennials because they killed the millennials off; they killed their future supporters off. They committed genocide among themselves. Pro-lifers tend to have more kids because the other side believes the myth of overpopulation and limit their numbers. They are jealous of the millennials—that we've got these pro-life kids that are very strong, very passionate. Millennials need to embrace the power that they already have—that they don't even understand that they have—and run with it.[24]

Jill has an excellent way of evaluating the various needs and projects within the pro-life movement. Her basic solution? *Act*. Do what you're passionate about, because it's all needed:

> The Bible says that we are a body, and the body is made up of many parts, and every part is just as important. The parts that are unseen are just as important as the parts that are seen, and all these body parts work together. And I think that can be applied to the pro-life movement. There are many different needs and many different components of the pro-life movement that all end up working together to achieve the goal of promoting a culture of life and making abortion not only unthinkable but also illegal.
>
> However a person feels impassioned to participate is where they should go, considering the time constraints they may have, the point in their life where they might be. . . . The needs are everywhere; they're all important.
>
> But the most important thing is *to get involved.* And not necessarily work too hard on making sure that you're in the right place, but just get involved and start investigating and start feeling things out. The first attempt that you make may not be where you end up, but you jump in and take it from there. The most important thing is getting in the game.[25]

The Pro-Life Wave: Bethany Goodman and Claire Chretien

In 2014, the national pro-life organization the Susan B. Anthony List recognized Bethany Goodman and Claire Chretien as two recipients of its Young Leader Award. Bethany and Claire were chosen for their "profound impact in the fight to protect preborn children and women" as part of "a new generation of trailblazers."[26] These young millennials are proof of proabortion leader Nancy Keenan's claim that "there are so many of them [pro-life activists], and they are so young."[27]

As a millennial Christian, Bethany determined that changing the current culture was her personal duty. Her work in the movement has been both steady and innovative as she's stretched across a number of spheres, including her local pregnancy resource center, Capitol Hill, the digital world, the March for Life Education and Defense Fund, and even work with underprivileged children in Washington, DC. She explained how she got involved in pro-life work:

> I became interested in cultural issues and current events because my parents taught my siblings and me to have a Christian worldview, to pay attention to the issues facing our community—and more broadly our country and world—and to be salt and light in those spheres, especially by loving our neighbors.
>
> I've never been able to recall a specific moment that sparked my concern about abortion or other justice issues, but for as long as I knew what abortion was, my heart was broken over it. . . . I wanted to do whatever I could to be an agent of change.[28]

Claire, a fellow millennial Christian, responded to the scientific facts and the looming injustice that faced her with action. Her passionate and determined efforts earned her college pro-life group the Students for Life of America's Group of the Year Award. Already experienced in media presentation and coalition building, Claire has a bright and visionary future ahead—exactly what America needs in the battle to end abortion. She says, "I became involved in fighting abortion with the goal of ending it right around the time I began college. I realized the profound injustice of abortion and discovered that the science of embryology clearly shows that humans are humans from the very beginning. At my first March for Life in 2012, I felt an intense calling to dedicate my life to ending abortion. Abortion is so unfair! I am consumed by an intense feeling—some days stronger than others, but always there nonetheless—that I must stop this injustice."[29]

Both Bethany and Claire remain inspired by their faith to protect preborn children. Bethany explains, "As Christians, we believe that people are created in the image of God, meaning that every person, no matter the circumstances of their birth, has value, dignity, and worth. Because of that truth, it is just and right to care for and protect every person, especially when they are most vulnerable, such as in the womb, orphaned, or impoverished."[30]

Claire describes the passion and absolute necessity behind such action: "The preborn are the most vulnerable and defenseless of our brothers and sisters. They are truly the 'least of these' who Jesus tells us to serve. As Christians, we must stand in solidarity with all people in need. No one is more in need than the preborn who are threatened by the brutal, torturous violence of abortion. The early Christians weren't afraid to tell the truth; we shouldn't be either. Abortion kills babies and hurts women."[31]

Bethany eloquently paints a picture of justice for the babies and women vulnerable to abortion: "First and foremost, preborn babies need the right to life. Justice for babies before birth would ultimately look like abortion being illegal, just as other forms of homicide, but until then, that means teaching justice to the culture. Moreover, women who face unexpected pregnancies need to be provided with the care and resources they need to choose life for their baby, and to say no to abortion, which will inflict physical, emotional, mental, and spiritual damage. Justice for these women looks like protection, care, resources, as well as love and support."[32]

Claire emphasizes the need for practical assistance and love for mothers: "Some [mothers] need practical assistance or a place to live. Some simply need an ear to listen and a friend to support them. Most importantly, mothers facing unexpected pregnancies need love, and so do their preborn children." She then offers advice for other millennials who want to get involved with ending abortion: "I recommend joining a student pro-life club, volunteering at a pregnancy center, going to the pro-life conferences organized by Students for Life of America, brushing up on pro-life apologetics, writing about abortion, and doing whatever you're good at to help the pro-life cause."[33]

Bethany reminds her fellow millennials that it's important to start doing justice *now*—whatever that looks like: "Start close to home. If there are families or individuals in your church, community, or workplace who are involved in the pro-life, foster care, and/or adoption movement or have personal experience, get to know them and their story. Follow good organizations on social media to get a daily feel for what they do, the people they help, and how you can get involved. You'll never be 100 percent 'ready' to begin making a difference, so find a local organization and start volunteering!"[34]

A Twenty-First-Century Defender: Seth Drayer

Since 2010, Seth Drayer has worked full time as a "preborn defender." Leading the charge as Created Equal's director of training and teaching students through programs at http://www.justiceride.org, Seth has debated university professors and appeared on national television. This former evangelical youth minister spends his time training students how to "intelligently respond to injustice":

> Created Equal [is] an organization dedicated to equipping students with the knowledge and conversational skills to create informed public debate about abortion. After training students to defend the humanity of preborn children and build a philosophic case for human equality, we pair these winsome apologists with

> visual evidence of abortion victims to create conversation on campus, in downtown squares, etc.
>
> We place photos and videos of abortion victims at the center of our demonstrations because abortion must be seen to be understood. How can we expect our society to reject the status quo if we deny them evidence of a grave injustice? . . . This is, ultimately, the victim's story.[35]

One of Seth's first public pro-life actions was giving a speech in high school:

> When I was in high school, I prepared a speech about abortion, and that led me to a video which showed the victims. I had never before seen what abortion does to preborn children. After watching the film, I grasped the barbarity of this injustice. I saw for myself how children are decapitated, dismembered, and disemboweled during routine abortions, and I knew I had to do something.
>
> Throughout my college years, I went with my aunt and cousins to an abortion facility to pray for women and men entering the building. And as I prayed for them, I also prayed God would give me an opportunity to do something to stop this injustice. And He did. I started helping to organize an apologetics camp for students who wanted to understand how to present the case for life [Life Defenders], joined the board of directors of Allen County Right to Life in Indiana, and utilized my role as a youth minister to lead youth in public demonstrations against abortion.

Seth came to the realization that as a church minister, he was a leader others would follow. He saw his position as both an opportunity and a responsibility to do justice for a group of human beings who are often neglected and left to die. Seth believes that the "pairing of abortion victim photos with respectful apologists" can "change minds on abortion."

Seth offers wise advice for any millennial who is wondering what he or she can do for preborn children. He also speaks to those who aren't particularly compelled by this justice issue, asking what an injustice of this magnitude means for each of us, despite our personal interests:

> For those interested in fighting abortion, I'd encourage them to frame this properly. There are two central questions to this debate: First, what is the preborn? And second, are we all created equal? If preborn embryos and fetuses are in fact humans, and if we are all equal, then to kill them for a reason we'd never kill born humans is blatant discrimination.
>
> I'd also encourage everyone . . . to consider what this injustice means for all of us . . . since this is an issue of human equality. . . . Once we strip human rights from one group of humans, all are vulnerable. . . . If all humans are not by definition valuable, we give terrible power to our leaders to determine who is and who is not worthy of life.
>
> The only way to achieve true justice is to recognize that all humans—black and white, rich and poor, born and preborn—are created equal.
>
> We must call for an end to this system by which nearly three thousand preborn babies are butchered every single day in our nation. Justice for them means recognizing the inherent rights they have as

image-bearers of God. It means ending the discrimination of killing human embryos and fetuses.[36]

Doing Justice

For specific action points, see Chapter Eleven. In this chapter, you'll also learn how to develop your own plan to do justice in this area. More resources, ideas, and information can be found at my Facebook page, https://www.facebook.com/KristiBurtonBrown/.

CHAPTER FOUR

Foster Care and Adoption Are Brave New Worlds

You will not stroll into Christlikeness with your hands in your pockets, shoving the door open with a careless shoulder. This is no hobby for one's leisure moments, taken up at intervals when we have nothing much to do, and put down and forgotten when our life grows full and interesting. . . . It takes all one's strength, and all one's heart, and all one's mind, and all one's soul, given freely and recklessly and without restraint.

—Arthur John Gossip

According to the Congressional Coalition on Adoption Institute, hundreds of thousands of American children have been abandoned, neglected, or abused and then absorbed into what we know as the foster care system. Approximately 397,122 children languish in the system right now, with 101,666 currently available for adoption.[1]

In 2007, the Casey Family Programs found that "about one-third of foster care alumni experienced three or more placement moves and an equal percentage (32.3%) experienced 8 or more placements throughout their child welfare careers."[2] These dire statistics prove that the needs of these children are not being met.

They are often well behind their peers emotionally, socially, and scholastically due to broken relationships, repetitive uprooting, the lack of a stable and protective home environment, and abuse. Every year, tens of thousands of children age out of the foster care system without committed parents, and the statistics do not bode well for their future success:

- In 2012, 23,396 youth aged out of the U.S. foster care system without the emotional and financial support necessary to succeed. Nearly 40 percent had been homeless or couch surfed, nearly 60 percent of young men had been convicted of a crime, and only 48 percent were employed. Seventy-five percent of women and 33 percent of men receive government benefits to meet basic needs. Fifty percent of all youth who aged out were involved in substance use, and 17 percent of the females were pregnant.[3]
- Nearly 25 percent of youth aging out did not have a high school diploma or GED, and a mere 6 percent had finished a two- or four-year degree after aging out of foster care. One study shows that 70 percent of all youth in foster care have the desire to attend college.[4]
- Thirty percent of abused and neglected children will later abuse their own children. Children who experience child abuse and neglect are 59 percent more likely to be arrested as a juvenile, 28 percent more likely to be arrested as an adult, and 30 percent more likely to commit a violent crime.[5]
- About 80 percent of abused children met the diagnostic criteria for at least one psychiatric disorder, including suicide attempts, depression, eating disorders, and so on, by the age of twenty-one.[6]

While the government is technically in charge of foster care, it is doing a poor job. The whole system should be reevaluated and reformulated. Currently, elected officials decide how much of a state's funding is spent in particular areas, and citizens can effectively organize, speak out, and bring issues to their officials' attention. There is a need for political advocates for children in the foster care system: "States spent a mere 1.2–1.3% of available federal funds on parent recruitment and training services even though 22% of children in foster care had adoption as their goal."[7]

Key issues include high turnover, lack of training, and lack of adequate payment for social or child welfare workers.[8] Special licensure and training is not always required, setting the system up for failure. All too often, the rights of caring parents are stripped away, while children suffering real abuse—at the hands of biological or foster parents—are overlooked.

To be a secure and successful network for abandoned children, more experts in social work and child welfare are required in the foster care system. Higher salaries should be offered, advanced training should be required and continually maintained, and available federal funds should be used in full. Better safeguards must be put in place so that abusers do not become foster parents. We cannot allow innocent children to continue to fall through the cracks of an inefficient and broken system. We also need more caring, competent individuals to volunteer as court-appointed special advocates who build relationships with children in foster care, make recommendations to the court for their well-being, and aid them in getting needed services that might otherwise be overlooked.[9]

The American Academy of Child and Adolescent Psychiatry reports that "most states encourage efforts to provide the birth parents with support and needed services (e.g., mental health or drug/alcohol treatment, parent skills, training and assistance with child care and/or adequate housing) so their child can be returned to them."[10] However, it's still a problem if most—but not *all*—states are doing this. If birth parents can become healthy, trained, and safe guardians, they are usually the best ones to raise their own children. Social justice advocates need to train and support parents and teach them how to meet the needs of their children. In fact, the biggest reason children are placed in foster care is not because of abuse but because of neglect and substance addiction.

In 2012 in Arizona, at least 59 percent of the children removed from their homes were taken away due to "drugs or alcohol use" that "were contributing factors to maltreatment."[11] ABC News reported that "most children are placed in foster care temporarily due to parental abuse or neglect. . . . Experts estimate that 80 to 90 percent of foster care placements can be traced to substance abuse."[12]

There is also an economic case to be made for investing in the youth trapped within the foster care system. In Ira Cutler's 2009 study, "Cost Avoidance: Bolstering the Economic Case for Investing in Youth Aging Out of Foster Care," he lays out the economic arguments in detail and also considers the higher rate of crime and lower rate of appropriate education for children in the foster care system. Cutler believes there is a way forward: "Tremendous [results] . . . can be achieved by providing effective services and supports and creating permanent relationships with responsible and caring adults. The tools exist to make improvements in the outcomes for aging out youth; all that is needed is the political will and leadership required to make the necessary investments."

Real-Life Justice Role Models

The following are the stories of some true social justice leaders who are seeking to make a difference.

A Modern-Day Reformer: Shelly Radic and Project 1.27

Shelly Radic has been on a crusade to improve the foster care system for years. Currently, she's the president of Project 1.27, a ministry based on James 1:27: "Religion that God our Father accepts as pure and faultless is this: to look after orphans and widows in their distress and to keep oneself from being polluted by the world." First a church ministry, Project 1.27 soon became a nonprofit organization, with operations in more than one hundred churches today. While foster families must still select a government or private agency to work with, Project 1.27 serves as a bridge that provides training for Christian families while inspiring them to truly serve these children.

Project 1.27 makes it possible for Christian families to meet the needs of neglected, abandoned, and abused children by caring for them with the heart of Christ. According to Shelly, Project 1.27 represents a way for the government and the faith community to work together to benefit needy children. County and private agencies also became involved as Project 1.27 took off:

> In 2004, Pastor [Robert] Gelinas realized there was a huge need for families in Colorado. There were 875 children in Colorado who were legally free, waiting for a family, and well over a thousand churches just in the Denver Metro area. He approached lieutenant governor Jane Norton, who had been tasked with solving this problem.
>
> The idea was, we noticed there was a barrier between foster care and the church. First, unawareness: How many children are waiting? And then, many didn't know what to do about it. Even if they called the county agencies, the employees there were often overworked. It could be difficult to find anyone to talk to, and there

> was also sometimes a disconnect between training and Biblical values.[13]

This merging of government resources and church action has been wildly successful. As of 2014—a mere decade after Project 1.27 was founded—the 875 waiting children have been reduced to 250. Shelly says, "Over 600 children have been placed in families . . . 275 adopted. We follow families for usually a couple years to make sure they have all they need. This is . . . something God has done through the collaboration of many organizations. There's been great work done that we'd love to see accomplished in other states and communities across the United States. There's a real need across the country for Christian families to step up and adopt our waiting children in foster care."[14]

Project 1.27 stands ready to help others form a similar ministry or organization in their own state. Shelly's deep involvement in this justice work stems from the fact that adoption and foster care are an integral part of her life. Her brother, husband, and two of her children are adopted—her brother from foster care. After twenty years of serving in Mothers of Preschoolers (MOPS), Shelly felt that God was calling her to something new, and with much prayer and seeking, foster care and adoption rose up in her heart once again. As she puts it, "God planted it in my heart from the very beginning of time."

Shelly explains why foster care is one of the premier social justice issues of our day:

> Many of the more recognized justice issues so often involve the kids in foster care who age out without a family. Up to 70 percent of people involved in trafficking were involved in foster care; over half of homeless people were involved in the child welfare system. At age twenty-five, the average person makes $26,000 a year . . .

> the average kid who ages out of foster care without a family makes about $6,000. Only 3 percent who age out ever graduate from college. Close to 70 percent graduate from high school by the time they're twenty-one, but it often takes until they're twenty-one because they have to keep restarting. Over half of the women who age out are pregnant by the time they're twenty-one . . . many of them . . . with their second child.
>
> I don't think a program can ever replace having a family . . . though there are good programs trying to take care of some these issues. When I think of our justice issues, they're often concerned with hunger, homelessness, and trafficking, and all of these are impacted by not having a family. Having a healthy, safe family is one of the best preventative measures against these issues . . . you belong somewhere, you have a place to sleep, your mom will give you some sandwiches, your grandmas will give you some money, your family will come around you. If you don't have this, you're easy prey.[15]

Shelly is convinced that Christians need to help these easily preyed upon children find the support—and the families—they so desperately need:

> One thing important to me when I started is that even though people realized this response to James 1:27—to care for, to look after orphans in their distress . . . I wanted them to know this wasn't a yes or no question. The answer's already yes. God's already told us yes, to do this. Our question should be how we should do this. An orphan is a child in need of protection and provision. In our country, it would be foster care. The Bible often

> talks about the fatherless . . . without a father, there was no one to provide protection or provision.
>
> Biblically, this is a social justice issue. God speaks about putting the lonely in homes, protecting the fatherless, and obviously, James 1:27. Clearly, this is something that God cares about deeply.[16]

Shelly offered advice for those who want to get involved with foster care—specifically, those who might not be able to care for a child in their own homes: "Look at the words 'come alongside.' Coach or mentor or befriend a child in foster care or a family in foster care. These kids are traumatized children who have a lot of grief and loss. Come alongside and pray. Come alongside and give to organizations. Come alongside and speak out for these kids. Tell your friends that we need to think about these kids. Prayerfully explore how God calls you to care for these kids and then be doers of the Word."[17]

An Open Invitation: Cana Brueckner

I met Cana Brueckner more than a decade ago, when we both attended a two-month Bible study and life skills course for young women. She stood out as a kind young woman who was always ready with a smile. Ten years later, we were both the mothers of two children each. For Cana and her husband, their precious sons came through an open invitation that they extended. The Brueckners adopted both of their boys, and the lessons they've learned apply to the closely related spheres of foster care and adoption.

The Brueckners' first son was domestically adopted in an open adoption. Open adoption allows the birth parents to be involved on whatever level is agreed upon by both families. Some birth parents receive monthly or yearly photos of their child as well as letters. Others visit the child frequently. It's essential that more people hear about this type of adoption. Many birth mothers are deeply saddened by the thought of putting their child out somewhere in the world where they believe they'll never know anything about him or her. And although this notion is based on old information, this is still the rap adoption often gets and one reason abortion is considered instead.

Christians like Cana and her husband put a face on open adoption and demonstrate that birth mothers can choose the parents of their child; they can choose to be involved in that child's life and always know just how he or she is doing. It's necessary for Christians to learn the facts about adoption and be familiar with beautiful stories like the Brueckners'.

With her second son, Cana extended yet another open invitation—this time from her womb. The Brueckners adopted their second son and five other embryos. The embryos were created from another couple's use of in vitro fertilization and were still frozen. "Snowflake adoption" is another little-known frontier that gives life to children who need parents. Through embryo adoption programs, embryos who have already been created and frozen are donated for adoption so that they, too, can be given a real chance at life. Nightlight Christian Adoptions "pioneered the first embryo donation and adoption program in the world and named it the Snowflakes Embryo Adoption Program."[18] As of early 2015, more than four hundred babies have been adopted and born through Nighlight's special program. The number exceeds six thousand when other programs are counted as well.

Cana was able to carry her second son for thirty-one weeks before he was born. She believes that adoption can prevent other injustices from happening to needy children: "When Christians ignore the responsibility of caring for orphans, the burden falls on unbelievers who don't have the Bible to keep them morally grounded. That has led to abortion, abusive foster homes, and starvation in parts of the world."[19] Cana doesn't believe, however, that every Christian must adopt a child personally to participate in doing justice. Instead, she shares a way that nearly every Christian can get involved:

> A huge need in the adoption world that I have experienced is sharing the financial burden. Even if you don't feel led to adopt personally, helping those who are is very important. Many people who adopt save for years, take out loans, max out credit cards, and use many more bad options because it is so hard to fund.
>
> It can be very hard for infertile couples to ask for help financially, emotionally, or otherwise. Since God has made a beautiful option for these couples in adoption, while at the same time saving His little ones, couples desperately need support and sometimes for others to help raise money or give.[20]

The Brueckners illustrate a quote from Martin Luther King Jr. that Cana loves: "Faith is taking the first step when you don't see the whole staircase."

Jumping in the River: Pastor Robert Gelinas

Pastor Gelinas is the lead pastor of Colorado Community Church in Aurora, Colorado, and the father of six children. One of his great passions is caring for orphans, and he is confident that God calls us to aid children who need foster care and adoption. Pastor Gelinas views this passion in a twofold way—as something he lives out in his personal life and as something he speaks out about as a pastor. He says, "It began as a personal journey for my wife and I, as we have six children. We adopted five of them—three from foster care and two from Ethiopia. That kind of gave way to recognizing that this was more than a personal calling but a professional calling because I'm a pastor. And that the church has a rightful role in foster and adoptive ministry."[21]

Realizing the church's rightful role led Pastor Gelinas to do more than simply open his mouth. It led him to act, founding and spearheading Project 1.27. A decade ago, when all this began, his dream was for every church: "If every church took one child, you'd have a waiting list of families and not a waiting list of children." Project 1.27 continues to work to make this dream a reality.

Pastor Gelinas was moved by the plight of orphans when he was just a young boy: "I was nine years old when I first read James 1:27, and it just was a normal part of the faith for me. Then fast forward when I get older and get married and we start having children, it just seemed like the obvious thing: there are children who need homes, and the Scripture's clear about it, so that's what we did. We had one child biologically and then said, we'll build our family through adoption from there on out."

Adoption and foster care boil down to one thing that all Christians are instructed to take part in: caring for orphans. According to Pastor Gelinas, it's definitely a matter of justice: "For me, it's a justice issue because every child deserves a home; every child deserves a family; every child deserves that, and when the one thing they should have been able to count on in life—and that was a mom and a dad—when that breaks down, justice is making sure that we do the best we can in providing that again. In the church, I think somehow these children would have that which was taken or lost restored in terms of the home and a family."

Pastor Gelinas considers the whole family where foster care and adoption is concerned. He insists that the birth parents, when possible, should also be cared for as a vital part of this process: "We have to make sure that we're not using the term *justice* the way the world does. . . . I would say that justice in the eyes of God would somehow include the birth parents as well and that they, too, can experience restoration because of the gospel. They're not the enemy in this; they're part of the need for justice and making things right in their life too."

Pastor Gelinas ranks an effective support system as the top requirement for families involved in foster care and adoption. This, he believes, is something any Christian can participate in, even if they are unable to foster or adopt personally: "The church is perfectly designed for adding support into the lives of people because churches know how to deal with pain. Churches deal with people in crisis all the time. When a church just takes on its natural way of supporting hurting and crisis people, then it works."

For millennial Christians who care about orphans, Pastor Gelinas has a unique suggestion:

> You don't have to wait until you get married to start caring for orphans. There's lots of ways to care: child sponsorship programs, or if you know a family that has adopted or fostered, becoming part of their support structure.
>
> One group of children in the foster care system that are oftentimes neglected are the seventeen- to eighteen-year-olds. And oftentimes, a single person can adopt that seventeen- or eighteen-year-old because they're going to graduate, they're going to move on to adulthood rather quickly. But at least that single person can now say, "You have a home," and "You have a mom," or "You have a dad." That leaves room then for the single person to still get married and build a family a different way but also provide a home. There's room for this kind of thinking.[22]

As demonstrated by his personal life, his sermons, and his ministry to orphans, Pastor Gelinas has taken the advice he gives others to heart. "Pastors," he says, "show people the river. Call people into the river. Jump into the river."[23] And with his family of six beautiful children and the continuation of Project 1.27, jumping is exactly what he's done.

Doing Justice

For specific action points, see Chapter Eleven. In this chapter, you'll also learn how to develop your own plan to do justice in this area. More resources, ideas, and information can be found at my Facebook page, https://www.facebook.com/KristiBurtonBrown/.

CHAPTER FIVE

Rescue

Human Trafficking and Slavery

Justice will not be served until those who are unaffected are as outraged as those who are.
—Benjamin Franklin

The Lord longs to be gracious to you. Therefore He will rise up to show you compassion for the Lord is a God of justice. Blessed are all who wait for Him!
—Isaiah 30:18

Human trafficking is one of the social justice issues that receives the most attention. And yet this great injustice still remains—partly because we have to deal with its many root causes, and that's a monstrous task. It's still important to rescue the people currently trapped in this enterprise, but until we reach in and yank out these roots—some of which are embedded deep in various societies and communities around the world—it will be impossible to stop the cycle.

For instance, in the United States (and perhaps elsewhere), a lot of human trafficking takes place where gambling takes place. It's also been proven that trafficked girls are often sold in business districts, where businessmen stay for short periods of time. Hotel workers in these areas must be trained how to identify trafficked girls and women and how to contact the proper authorities that can rescue them. Sex slavery comes to town along with huge sporting events—like the Super Bowl and the Olympics. Prior to these events, people in these cities should be trained on identification and rescue. Churches should collect additional volunteers to work in the city during this time.

Liz Yore, whose amazing work you will read about later in this chapter, explains the root causes of trafficking and presents some options to combat it:

> Human trafficking is driven by poverty, dysfunction, pornography, money, abortion, and evil. Each one of these conditions needs to be addressed in order to end human trafficking. I believe that governments and NGOs should focus on prevention of human trafficking. Once victims are lured into slavery, it is extremely difficult to extricate them from this violent and psychological web of dependence. Tragically, trafficking is big business, pursued by the mafia, criminal gangs, terrorists, and street thugs. Until demand is reduced, trafficking will continue to flourish . . . Finally, financial support should be used for victim services. Presently, government funds are largely targeting conferences and not reaching the real victims of human trafficking.[1]

Human trafficking, like abortion, continues in part because it is a largely hidden injustice. Groups like Exodus Cry believe that the reality of human trafficking and sex slavery must be brought to the forefront of people's minds on a consistent basis; social awareness must occur so that culture changes and people act to stop—and prevent—this injustice.

For years, Polaris Project has been a trusted source of information on the human trafficking industry. The organization does an excellent job of combing through and reporting on data from government agencies and child advocacy organizations. In June 2015, Polaris released the report "Child Trafficking and the Child Welfare System," which demonstrates that many areas of injustice are interconnected. The failings of the foster care system have created an open market for traffickers who prey on vulnerable children and teens.

The following are statistics from the Polaris report:

- One in six runaways in 2014 were likely sex trafficking victims. Of these, 68 percent were in the care of social services or foster care when they ran.
- In 2014, 130 victims of sex trafficking were identified in Connecticut. Of these, 98 percent were involved with the child welfare system in some manner.
- Of the child advocacy centers in the Midwest region, 74 percent have served commercial sexual exploitation of children (CSEC) victims. However, only 13 percent had policies and procedures in place specific to CSEC needs, and 91 percent of respondents reported having no funding for CSEC victims.[2]

A major roadblock in fighting the human trafficking industry is the fact that many people who could be rescuing the victims haven't been taught how to recognize or help them. Things are certainly improving, but a huge training deficit remains. Hotel workers; law enforcement officers; medical staff at hospitals, clinics, and doctors' offices; and child welfare workers all need to be trained on identifying and appropriately aiding human trafficking victims. Since many victims are unable to escape on their own, they need advocates in these professions who can help rescue them.

As Polaris puts it, "Victims of sex trafficking routinely interacted with people outside their trafficking situations who were in positions to provide assistance."[3] Lauren, who survived her trafficking ordeal, shared that even though she went "to hospitals, urgent care clinics, women's health clinics, and private doctors," no one bothered to ask about her situation or find out what was going on.[4] Even though "most [human trafficking] survivors [87.8 percent] did receive medical treatment at some point during their trafficking . . . studies have demonstrated that medical care providers are woefully unprepared to identify trafficking victims."[5]

According to data collected by Polaris, the National Human Trafficking Resource Center, and the BeFree Textline, the primary venues of commercial sex (in order) are hotels and motels, the street, residential brothels, escort/delivery services, porn, hostess/strip clubs, truck stops, commercial front brothels, and bars/clubs.[6]

More work must also be done to find traffickers based on their online presence. Polaris reports that traffickers can advertise all over the web, often without exposing their identity:

> One website which advertises commercial sex services listed nearly 12,000 ads nationwide for these services on a single day in 2014.
>
> Purchasers of commercial sex use online forums to review their experiences and spread information about how to avoid law enforcement detection. Traffickers may also use the social media posts of victims to monitor their activities or track their location.[7]

Polaris is an essential resource in the fight against trafficking. Its website is full of useful information, including graphics that identify common risk factors for trafficking victims. Internationally, women—and particularly young girls—are trafficked by their own families in addition to strangers. Virgins bring a good price, and parents are willing to sell their daughters to improve their dire financial straits and overwhelming poverty. "The Women Who Sold Their Daughters into Sex Slavery," an expose from the CNN Freedom Project, sheds light on this stunning practice.[8] It also tells the story of Don Brewster, a former pastor who, with his wife, Bridget, moved to "the epicenter of child trafficking" in Cambodia. The Brewsters run Agape International Mission (AIM)[9] and go inside brothels to talk with young trafficked girls and rescue them. CNN describes AIM as "an organization dedicated to rescuing and rehabilitating the victims of child trafficking in Cambodia and smashing the networks that exploit them."

The U.N.'s 2014 report on human trafficking explained one reason the Brewsters' work produces results: "Responses . . . need to be tailored to national and regional specifics if they are to be effective, and if they are to address the particular needs of victims, who may be child soldiers or forced beggars, or who may have been enslaved in brothels or sweatshops."[10] The report also revealed the following statistics about trafficking between 2010 and the present:

- There have been at least 510 trafficking routes detected.
- Approximately 72 percent of convicted traffickers are men, and 28 percent are women. This represents a much higher crime rate than women normally have.
- Out of all detected victims, 49 percent are adult women and 33 percent are children. This is a 5 percent increase in child victims compared to the 2007–10 period.
- The rate of underage girls in the share of trafficking has increased from 10 percent in 2004 to 21 percent in 2011. The rate of underage boys has risen from 3 percent to 12 percent in the same time period.
- More than six out of ten of all victims have been trafficked across at least one national border.

- Out of every three child victims, two are girls, and one is a boy.
- Some victims are trafficked by their own family members.
- Trafficked people worldwide included 49 percent women, 18 percent men, 21 percent girls, and 12 percent boys (2011).[11]

The report identified the purposes of trafficking throughout the world as "sexual exploitation, organ removal, forced labour, servitude, and slavery," among others. The creation of child soldiers is another trafficking issue in some areas of the world.

It is difficult to determine the exact number of people who are trapped in trafficking, at risk for trafficking, or trafficked each year in the United States and abroad. However, the U.S. Department of Homeland Security estimates that "as many as 100,000–300,000 American children are at risk of being trafficked for commercial sex in the United States" each year.[12]

In 2012, the Associated Press (AP) stated that the U.N. crime-fighting office revealed that, internationally, the victims of human trafficking are estimated at 2.4 million.[13] The AP also reported that a U.N. official claimed that there was $32 billion "being earned every year by unscrupulous criminals running human trafficking networks" and that only 1 percent of the victims are rescued. The U.N. recognizes that human beings have become products, like drugs and weapons. To add to the problem, only a small minority of police units are trained to specifically deal with trafficking.

Like many justice issues, human trafficking is interconnected with other violations. Pimps often take their captive women to abortion clinics—Planned Parenthood in particular. Genevieve Plaster of the Charlotte Lozier Institute discussed the findings of Dr. Laura Lederer, a former senior advisor for trafficking in persons for the U.S. Department of State and founder of the nonprofit Global Centurion. Testifying before a U.S. House subcommittee, Lederer called forced abortion a "trend in sex trafficking,"[14] as it proves to be yet another way to control and endanger the victims. According to Lederer's study, 55 percent of female sex slaves had at least one abortion, and 30 percent had several. She said, "Notably, the phenomenon of forced abortion in sex trafficking transcends the political boundaries of the abortion debate, violating both the pro-life belief that abortion takes innocent life, and the prochoice ideal of women's freedom to make their own reproductive choices."[15]

Live Action, an investigative human rights organization, conducted an inquiry and found Planned Parenthood clinics around the nation willing to work with pimps to give "services" to trafficked girls.[16] Planned Parenthood failed to appropriately report the pimps for what they were doing, even when underage girls were involved. Human trafficking expert Dottie Laster wrote of Live Action's investigative videos: "After viewing the Planned Parenthood video my first thoughts were of the victims I have served over the last 8 years. Specifically the women and girls—their horrendous statements of rape, gang rapes, torture, branding, starvation, extortions, assault and their reports of repeated forced abortions and miscarriages due to the trauma they received. I have often wondered where these multiple abortions took place and how medical professionals had not seen the extensive trauma to their bodies, spirits, and souls."[17]

In early September 2015, Alliance Defending Freedom released a thirteen-page summary detailing how in seven states across the nation, Planned Parenthood has been caught sending victims of sexual abuse back to their abusers after performing and charging for an abortion.[18] In one case, "the child was taken to three different abortion facilities, including a Planned Parenthood facility. Given that the abuse continued for years it is evident that none of the abortion facilities made a report to law enforcement. This tragic case is an outstanding example of how the failure of many people, including Planned Parenthood employees, resulted in a child being raped for years."[19] These facts demonstrate why Planned Parenthood is not a valid "women's health care provider" worthy of taxpayer dollars.

In the United States, Planned Parenthood is complicit in human trafficking—whether negligently or intentionally—as it sometimes fails to alert authorities to dangerous predators and traffickers. Dr. Laura Lederer reports that 29.6 percent of trafficking survivors claimed to have visited a Planned Parenthood, and yet it was not Planned Parenthood that helped them escape their abuse. Lederer also shares the story of a survivor who had one or more of her six abortions at Planned Parenthood "because they didn't ask any questions."[20]

Steven Wagner, former director of the Human Trafficking Program at the U.S. Department of Health and Human Services, explains how forced abortions—a common occurrence in the trafficking world—are often a "death sentence" for the victims. Forced abortions push them back to sexual slavery faster, as these women—who are sold as young as fourteen—are mere money-making products. Wagner explains that on average, the victims die by the age of twenty-one. He says, "The mortality rate for someone in commercial sexual exploitation is 40 times higher than for a non-exploited person of the same age. Helping a victim return to exploitation more quickly by terminating a pregnancy increases the odds of death."[21]

As Plaster puts it, "These instances of forced abortion [during human trafficking] cover the crimes, allow for ongoing abuse, and further rob the victim of any sense of humanity as that humanity in her womb is also snuffed out."[22]

Real-Life Justice Role Models

I have had the privilege of interviewing several warriors for justice who are standing up in our generation. Here are their stories.

Freedom in the Truth: Elizabeth "Liz" Yore

You've already read Liz Yore's take on the root causes of human trafficking at the beginning of this chapter. She is convinced that we must not only rescue people once they've been enslaved but act to *prevent* trafficking.

Few are as experienced as Liz in issues of trafficking. She has served in many influential positions throughout her life, including special counsel at Harpo Inc.; member of the Oprah Winfrey Leadership Academy for Girls in South Africa; general counsel for the Illinois Department of Children and Family Services, where she created the first missing child unit (with special provisions for missing foster kids) and aggressively prosecuted human trafficking cases; and general counsel at the National Center for Missing and Exploited Children in Virginia, where she also served as the first director of the international division.

You could say that when it comes to human trafficking—especially of children—Liz knows what she's talking about. She currently consults internationally in child exploitation cases, and you can connect with her on her blog, https://yorechildren.com, or on Twitter, @ElizabethYore. Liz was inspired by her own kids to fight for the children of the world:

> My children inspired me to get involved in the work of child protection. Their courage, honesty, and innocence opened my eyes and heart to understand that the dignity of the child is the most important tenet of a civilized society.
>
> Throughout the New Testament, Christ teaches that unless we become like little children, we will not enter the kingdom of heaven. Christ repeatedly admonishes the crowds and his disciples to become like little children. For me, as I chased evil predators during the

> course of my legal career, I ironically saw the importance of innocence. We, as adults, and society as a whole, have lost our way by casting off the most important of virtues: innocence.[23]

She reveals important information about boys, foster children, and trafficking:

> In 2005, as general counsel of the Illinois Department of Children and Family Services, I formed a partnership with the Chicago FBI office under the Innocence Lost Initiative to investigate and prosecute traffickers that preyed on children in foster care. It was the first federal prosecution and conviction under the human trafficking law. There were additional cases of trafficking involving foster children in an international ring, which resulted in their recovery and return to the United States. Based on my experience, while human trafficking primarily involves women victims, traffickers do not solely target females. Boys are victims of traffickers and, increasingly, women are involved as pimps and traffickers. Modern slavery impacts both sexes as victims and perpetrators. Human trafficking is exploding globally for a whole host of reasons, and few inroads are made to effectively rescue victims.

Liz has great advice for millennials and any "average, caring citizen" desiring to work for justice in the trafficking world:

> Millennials should immerse themselves in learning about these issues. It is critical that they pray first, then act. God will put people and opportunities in your path. The scourge of human trafficking demands an army of [people] to take up arms against modern slavery. Look

> at the success of the Mothers Against Drunk Drivers (MADD) movement. These mothers transformed the culture, the dialogue, the laws and policies against driving while drunk in a few short decades. There is a zero tolerance for drinking and driving in society.
>
> Look at the movement to find missing children in the United States. New laws, resources, and technology was initiated and demanded by parents of missing children. They turned their sorrow into power. The Amber Alert, the Age Progression Technology, Missing Children posters were ideas promulgated by average, caring citizens who believed they could solve and find missing children.
>
> We can never underestimate the imaginative power and commitment of the youth to solve critical social problems. All that is necessary is the willingness and heart to take up the cause.[24]

Liz believes that because each person is made in the image of God, one of the greatest things someone can do is "save the life of a child, rescue a human trafficking victim, or elevate human dignity in society."

Not Enough Time to Quit: Tom Tillapaugh

Tom Tillapaugh, president of the StreetSchool Network, found his calling to work against human trafficking in a pretty scary way: he almost died. This is one reason Tom believes we simply don't have enough time in this life to quit working for justice:

> I had open heart surgery in 1980, but the stitching of my artificial valves was being eaten away for years. The cardiologist ended up wanting to replace the valve, as a redo is really hard because of scar tissue. I went in, and

> during the surgery, I had a stroke. Calcification went through my system and killed brain cells. I was in a coma for five days, had to relearn how to tie my shoes and some speaking. I asked, "Lord, why did You let me live? What more do You have for me to do?"[25]

After Tom's recovery, a woman from Florida contacted him:

> I teach people how to start their own schools all over the country. A woman in Florida asked me to help her start a school for girls who were rescued from sex trafficking. She explained how bad and how pervasive it is in the US—even our girls are being [trafficked]. American men selling American women to American men.
>
> The average age of entry into sex trafficking in America is twelve to thirteen years old. The weird thing is, it's statutory rape unless money exchanges hands. Then it's prostitution. The guy gets a year in jail, if that, and the punishment is focused on the girl. It's all backward, all wrong.

Tom also learned that trafficking centers are often not located in areas that people would expect, and the men who buy the girls are often ordinary looking, professional white guys or people who have the money to attend big sporting events:

> In the Denver metro area, the center is in the Denver Tech Center. White suburban businessmen. Jefferson County is huge too. Downtown—by Mile High Stadium, the Marriot. There's also online: Backpage.com, the adult section, escorts. You buy a car or a little girl. Per capita, Colorado Springs—Cheyenne Mountain and the Broadmoor area—is worse than Denver. Again,

> white suburban men who have the money are the johns, typically.
>
> Think about the places girls are brought in to—the Super Bowl, Stock Show, Olympics, et cetera. That means sports fans as well as the wealthier and higher-up people in our society are raping little girls.

If you ever sit down with Tom, you'll see he gets right to the point and isn't afraid to speak the horrific truth about the worst parts of our world. He'll tell you exactly how it is, shedding light on the real reasons Christians can't be silent about the complete evil that is human trafficking. Tom explains that gangs have changed their priorities, now focusing on selling girls instead of drugs. Some girls are kidnapped, but most are groomed. During the grooming process, these girls—who often come from dysfunctional homes or are without a father—are made to feel special and wanted. Usually the pimps, posing as a new boyfriend or a good friend, will eventually take the girl to a party where she will be gang-raped and initiated into the trafficking world. The effects are devastating, as Tom details: "The average life-span for a trafficked girl or woman is seven years. They often die, or they are so destroyed that they keep going even when the pimp gets rid of them. The girls/women have a quota every night. If they don't meet it, they are starved, beaten, or made to go back out."[26]

Tom started a home for trafficked girls in Colorado called Hope Academy. It opened its doors in the summer of 2015. Denver probation asked Tom if they could send him girls they found who were recovering from sex trafficking. He says that most of the girls in Denver were African American and Hispanic, and many had been treated as the lowest on the totem pole, told they were ruined, and had their education taken from them. Tom knew these girls needed "quality academic education, vocational training, work readiness, entrepreneurship, trauma counseling, [and] financial literacy." When the probation staffers told him that the girls had no hope left, Tom knew that because "the Lord makes something from nothing," he would call the school Hope Academy and believe that God would restore the hope that had been stolen. He was committed to building a Christian environment with Christian teachers and counselors for the girls so they could truly grow.

Tom could talk about all aspects of trafficking for hours. He is a wealth of information on the topic, and I was riveted to his descriptions of how we need to improve our society. More pastors need to hold fundraisers or events to educate about human trafficking—like a group of pastors in Lakewood, Colorado, have done. More victims need to be rescued from the truck stops, where they are often dropped off by their pimps and called "Lock Lizards." Law enforcement needs better training, more staff, and more resources. Hotels need to become willing partners in curbing the sex trafficking trade.

Tom spoke of cops becoming the rescuers instead of the arresters of trafficked girls, and he was proud to tell me of a county in Colorado and an FBI agent he has worked with who do it right. He spoke of getting to the eight-year-old boys who are vulnerable to becoming pimps and raising them right. Tom pointed to the Sacred Heart School for boys in Washington, DC, as an example. He wants to see more schools around the nation that raise up poor kids to break the cycle so they can become good parents themselves. Tom knows we need more homes for trafficked girls that provide education for them during the day and a safe place to stay at night. He also believes that laws should be pointed in the right direction—not at the trafficked, but at the ones buying and selling them.

There's so much work to be done, as Tom will no doubt tell you. But, as he would also say, there is hope. The tide is turning, and as long as we take the initiative to enact change, it will keep turning.

Every Person Should Be Free: Blaire Pilkington Fraim

With the rallying cry "Every person should be free," Exodus Cry "combine[s] prayer and practical ministry to see sex trafficking and slavery ended around the world."[27] Exodus Cry "harnesses the power of film" to help people visualize the realities of human trafficking with their own eyes. What you see is hard to deny.

Blaire Pilkington, former director of intervention at Exodus Cry, describes this ministry's core vision: "Exodus Cry is a Christ-centered organization committed to the abolition of commercial sexual exploitation. We accomplish this through two targeted focuses: our abolition work which focuses on prayer, reform, and prevention; and our work to intervene on behalf of victims and see them restored." A devoted Christian millennial, Blaire was motivated to take up her cross on this issue as a teenager. She explains how she realized the gravity and breadth of this injustice:

> I was nineteen years old and a missionary with Youth With A Mission in Cambodia when I was first exposed to victims of sex trafficking. I remember seeing young Khmer girls on "dates" with older, foreign men. This led me on a journey throughout college to begin to understand that this wasn't only a "Cambodia issue" but a global system of injustice grossing billions of dollars each year. Upon finishing university, I moved to the International House of Prayer in Kansas City where Exodus Cry was just in its infancy. God began to mark my heart in a considerable way in the place of prayer, and I began to volunteer with the organization, which led to a full-time position that I've had the privilege of walking in for almost six years.[28]

After six years of experience, Blaire is well equipped to describe the great need for her fellow millennials—and all followers of

Christ—to educate themselves and act against human trafficking: "The systems of injustice that pervade our culture today and perpetuate this crime are wide spread and well networked. In order to effectively combat this illicit trade in human life, we must have a unified and committed response that spans many fields and spheres of influence. There is no community, sphere of influence, or field of work that is excluded from the reach of trafficking. There is a great amount of work to do, and it starts with becoming educated about the issue and then taking your passions, influence, finances, time, and prayers and lending them toward a solution."

Quoting Matthew 16, "The gates of hell will not prevail against the church," Blaire believes that Christians need to "exercise our authority in the place of prayer, get equipped with the facts, choose action over passivity and silence, and be the hands and feet of Christ reaching to those most vulnerable and effected by this system of injustice." As the church acts, Blaire is confident that "we will see light overcome darkness in our communities, captives set free and restoration."

Blaire describes how the people of God can act not only to rescue enslaved people but also to prevent trafficking from happening in the first place: "I believe justice for these victims looks like family. Most of these women and children are trafficked because they were vulnerable. That starts in the home. Often it is the breakdown of the family compounded by poverty and sexual abuse that makes these ones so vulnerable to trafficking. We are called to function as the family of God to those who have not known love, safety, and protection. Freedom, healing, and justice looks like a family. A place where they are safe, fed, loved unconditionally, invested in, and encouraged to dream again."

Blaire believes that preventing, rescuing, and restoring is a mission from the heart of Christ and central to the gospel itself: "In Luke 4, Jesus clearly describes His mission . . . The liberation of the poor and oppressed is central to the gospel. What hope do victims of human trafficking have apart from the hope of Jesus Christ to not only deliver them physically but also to heal the trauma and pain of the exploitation they have suffered in? We in the church are the exclusive carriers of this message and not only have a responsibility but also the authority to see these systems of injustice overturned and individual lives set free."

Blaire offered this advice for millennials who want to remove the scourge of trafficking and slavery:

> Seek Him first. Open your ears, hear what God is saying—what's on His heart and how He is calling you to respond. Strategies are released in the place of prayer. God wants to use our lives, He wants to partner with us. Don't run out ahead with your good intentions and ideas. Wait in the place of prayer and let Him send you out! As He begins to release strategies, pay attention to your passions.
>
> If you are an artist, create art that brings awareness to human trafficking. If you are a techie person, develop technology that tracks traffickers and their online activities, which are often traceable. If you want to work with victims, pursue a degree in psychology or social work. Finally, get equipped and learn from others who have been in this field longer—who have made mistakes but who have continued to persevere.[29]

Doing Justice

For specific action points, see Chapter Eleven. In this chapter, you'll also learn how to develop your own plan to do justice in this area. More resources, ideas, and information can be found at my Facebook page, https://www.facebook.com/KristiBurtonBrown/.

CHAPTER SIX

The Real War on Women

The Plight of Women Worldwide

O LORD, be gracious to us; we long for you. Be our strength every morning, our salvation in time of distress.
—ISAIAH 33:2

In America, many outraged about the "War on Women" don't seem to know what a war really is. If we want to fight a real war, we will fight against the systems that subject women and girls to child marriage, systemic rape, brutalization, honor killings, forced abortions, female gendercide, female circumcision/mutilation, and human trafficking.

The shocking things that women around the world are subjected to sound a little more warlike than dealing with American employers who decline to pay for birth control that violates their religious beliefs by causing chemical abortions. What kind of difference could we make if we focused on ending domestic violence in America and giving women and mothers real tools to get themselves—and their children—out of abusive situations? What kind of justice could we bring if we looked outside America and focused on countries where women are trampled down, forced into silence, and regularly abused?

What if we focused on giving *real* health care to women with medical problems? Take, for example, the problem of fistulas. In impoverished or undeveloped nations, many women—a large percentage of them child brides and/or women who were subjected to genital mutilation—suffer from this condition. Girls Not Brides explains how fistulas cause women to continually leak urine or feces.[1] The pain can be almost unbearable, and the women have to live with a constant, embarrassing odor. Sometimes they are rejected by their husbands and even their parents, and often, they lose their babies during a dangerous labor and delivery. In addition to inflicting physical pain, fistulas can cause women to lose everyone who is dear to them.

According to a report by *WorldPost*, South Sudan is one of the most dangerous environments for women.[2] Lack of education, lack of access to health care, and a distrust of medicine have combined with frequent conflict and crushing poverty to cause a high mortality rate among teenage girls. *WorldPost* describes the U.N. finding that "South Sudanese girls are three times more likely to die in childbirth than to enter high school." Sadly, South Sudan is not an isolated example. The BBC reported on widespread tragedy in another African nation, the Democratic Republic of Congo, where "an average of 48 women and girls are raped every hour."[3]

Voice of the Martyrs tells the story of Ruth, an Egyptian woman who was subjected to kidnapping, rape, nearly being sold into marriage, rejection and shaming by her family, and finally, an "honor killing" carried out by her own mother and brother after she converted from Islam to Christianity.[4] This is what war sounds like. If we care about ending the *real* War on Women, we must focus on true justice issues, like the ones Ruth—and so many violated women around the world—face daily.

As the founder and president of Live Action, Lila Rose advocates for compassionate care for vulnerable women of all ages, including the preborn girls. She shares some remarkable insights on justice for women around the world. It's clear, according to Lila, that women's rights are deeply threatened by radical Islamic subjugation of women or where "culturally, because of the caste system and other factors, women are facing a lack of protection, or their rights not being respected." She defines women's rights as "at the core . . . equal dignity to men; to be treated with equal protection to men under any law."

While many believe that equality means that men and women have no real differences, Lila recognizes that in order to truly support women and advance their equality, we must embrace the differences between the genders:

> Women's rights also involve ensuring that we recognize . . . the unique qualities that women bring. Sometimes these qualities require special treatment to give women the support that they need, whether it's from the business that they're involved in or from their church. There needs to be a recognition of their status as mothers and how that will impact the education and daily lives of their children. A recognition of the differences needs to be front and center in the dialogue on how we create a society of strong families. Tragically, instead of having these conversations, countries like China are not only failing to have these conversations, but they're actually trying to squash and terrorize women's rights, especially in the area of our amazing ability to bring children into the world.

Lila explains that in the United States, the view that legalized abortion has forced on women and on society's view of women has deeply damaged us all:

> It's extremely tragic and unjust that women who are pregnant are not seen as the guardians of another person, but instead, they're seen as one body and one person alone, and that extra person and body—their preborn child—is not recognized. [This] . . . makes the child a burden and totally places the burden of that child on the woman, because the law and society is not even recognizing that child.
>
> When we throw around the slogan "Your body, your choice" to women, this translates into "It's your body; it's your problem." And what that does is force women into a horrific situation where they are providing the future of the country through children, but they're being completely cut down in that amazing gift that they're giving the nation and their families. They're being told that it doesn't matter; we don't care, you deal with it. And that's one of the reasons we have over a million abortions a year in the US alone—precisely because we say your body your choice; your body, your problem.

Jesus was revolutionary in His time for seeing women not as problems or property to be used and dismissed but as valuable, worthy people created in the image of God. Jesus willingly touched and healed the woman with the issue of blood (Matt. 9:20–22; Mark 5:25–34; Luke 8:43–48)—an untouchable—in front of an entire crowd, calling her "daughter."

Two of our Savior's valued friends were women, the sisters Mary and Martha. He was not afraid to buck the customs of His day when these conventions oppressed and belittled others in unbiblical ways (Luke 7:36–50; Matt. 15:21–28; Mark 7:24–30; John 4:1–42). Jesus recognized the great bond women have with their children, both in His own life, and in the lives of others. In Nain (Luke 7:11–17), while Jesus was being followed by a great multitude, He stopped to tell a widow to "weep not" over the death of her only child as Jesus raised him from the dead. And on the cross, one of Jesus's few statements included assigning His disciple John as His beloved mother's new caregiver and protector.

Phillip Yancey once observed, "For women and other oppressed people, Jesus turned upside down the accepted wisdom of his day. According to biblical scholar Walter Wink, Jesus violated the mores of his time in every single encounter with women recorded in the four gospels."[5] Jesus continually took time to stop, see women for who they really were, speak kindly to them, meet their needs, and love them. He brought them justice. He brought them healing. He brought them compassion in a world that devalued them. And ultimately, He brought them salvation.

The landscape of justice for women is broad. It stretches from our own neighborhood to the farthest foreign city. There is the woman in church who is being secretly abused and doesn't know how to escape with her children. She fears telling the truth to friends or law enforcement because she has been trained to think that something worse will happen if she speaks up.

There is the fourteen-year-old girl, trapped in a polygamous Mormon community, about to be "married" and raped by a man forty years her senior.

There is the trafficked girl, kidnapped by a guy in his twenties who pretended to care about her, stowed away in our city's business district, being abused with no end in sight.

There are the women dying, suffering mutilation, being forced into slavery and unwanted marriages, and being undeservedly punished simply for being women in more countries and cities and villages than we can count.

There are the teenage girls in war-torn nations being stolen away as the property of their oppressors, used and abused as the Islamic "right" of men, simply because they have the XX chromosome.

There are the baby girls being drowned in buckets of water or being abandoned to be eaten by wild animals in the forests simply because they were created female.

These are the injustices we must stop. This is the War on Women we need to end.

Liz Yore, whom we met in Chapter Five, explains the issues women face: "The most important justice issue for women today is the hypersexualization of the culture and denigration of the dignity of the human being. All the resulting crimes of domestic violence, sexual assault, trafficking, pornography, etc. flow from these issues. Girls and women are always the first and primary victims of societal abuse. The genesis of this degradation is abortion and, until abortion ends, the human family of men, women and children will continue to be victimized."

Sarah Ray, an American entrepreneur who cofounded Yobel Market (a company that buys and sells goods made by women around the world) and its nonprofit arm, Yobel International, explains what she believes are the needs of women around the world:

> I think women everywhere are most in need of understanding their identity as one who is beloved and chosen by Christ. We are in need of knowing that we are worthy of love and dignity, and we need the societies we belong within to uphold these values and basic human rights. It starts there.
>
> Next, I think women are in need of healing—primarily from the trauma that so many of us have faced. . . .

> I also believe that women are in need of . . . men of integrity in their lives and communities. I believe they are in need of governments that uphold their rights as equals to men.[6]

Sarah also speaks of the need for educational and vocational opportunities for women:

> As women are educated more consistently, social and political change are inevitable as the values that women hold dear are then more often represented communally and civically.
>
> Lastly, when women are empowered to generate income, 90 percent of what they earn remains in the family. This means that their children will receive quality nutrition and education and will be protected from exploitative forms of labor. This results in systemic change for the next generation, and nations can move forward.[7]

Justice for women will come through cultural reform, individualized help, and most of all, the gospel.

Real-Life Justice Role Models

The following are the stories of some true social justice leaders who are seeking to make a difference.

One-Girl Revolution: Kate Bryan

Kate Bryan is an up-and-coming women's leader in media and social justice. Currently a senior account executive at CRC Public Relations, Kate was the past director of communications at the American Principles Project. Her résumé speaks of her faithfulness to the fight for justice. She's worked for an Irish senator, Live

Action, and the Life Institute in Dublin. Her words are published in several media outlets—including *Time*, *Breitbart*, *The Federalist*, and *Accultured*—and she has also appeared on television, broadcasting the fact that *true* feminism is owned by conservatives.

Kate gives an eye-opening and thoughtful take on politics and culture, specifically as they relate to women. Her New Year's resolution? To be a "real one-girl revolution."[8] She identifies the need to empower women with self-worth and self-respect: "We need to promote within girls, from a young age, that they are beautiful, unique, amazing individuals, and we need to teach them to believe it." She continues, "No matter what the world tries to instill within this woman, she will have the truth ingrained within her that she is an amazing and beautiful woman with the power to change the world. It wouldn't take much to change the world if we changed how our young girls saw themselves."

Kate also believes that young women need to continue to challenge cultural standards that define what it means to be a woman: "People used to challenge films, music, and so on that degraded women—but now, these things are celebrated. The culture tells us women have the right to take off their clothes on television and that there's something empowering about women being the object in sex scenes in movies. What ever happened to 'Women deserve better' or 'Women are more than just their bodies'? In this way, we really have backtracked, and there's no longer respect for women or their bodies or an understanding that women truly can change the world."[9]

Kate's inspiration for getting involved with the pro-life movement was her mother, who taught her that "every life is precious and that women are powerful and amazing creatures who can create new life and change the world." In her view, abortion not only kills children but tears apart the lives of mothers and fathers.

Kate also notes that her attention has shifted toward women facing a crisis in their pregnancies:

> I've seen the negative effects that abortion has had on women in my life, and wish that I could take that pain away or help them move through it. I've seen first-hand that there is nothing empowering about abortion; it's something that negatively affects women for the rest of their lives. Even if they can find healing and move beyond it, their abortion always stays with them.
>
> Women deserve better than abortion, and I'm still looking forward to the day when Gloria Steinem, Cecile Richards, Lena Dunham, and other so-called women's rights activists will recognize that.

In addition, Kate shared how our knowledge of injustice requires us to step up and take responsibility. She describes how we can make changes in our daily lives to bring justice to women:

> Every woman has the power to change the way the world sees women, and they can do it simply by living their lives in a respectable and fascinating way. Women are fascinating and amazing—let's start acting like it. Second, it has to do with each person, male and female, and how we see women. If we see women for their true worth and treat them accordingly, that will have a domino effect with the rest of society. All it takes is one person to shift the perspective of another, and this can be done simply through our daily lives. Women, respect yourselves and know that you are amazing. . . . Everyone, treat women as your sisters, mothers, friends . . . if you treat every woman that way, it will have a lasting effect in those women's lives, but also on the rest of society.

According to Kate, when the world sees Christians act on behalf of justice, it will follow suit:

> Christians have a responsibility to set an example for the rest of the world in all things. Christians, in particular, need to not only talk about their beliefs but also set a good example in their daily lives. . . . Christians have a responsibility to live their lives as an example, to speak up and to be active against matters of abuse, violence, and other social justice issues. If Christians would set an example in all things, the world would follow suit. The problem is that Christians often find it easier to live in their comfortable daily lives and only speak up when it's convenient. That's not what we need these days. We need revolutionaries and martyrs for the faith.

I'm often inspired by Kate's writing, as she reminds me of the need to do what we can for justice, whether it's big or small in our eyes. Justice matters—wherever and whenever we can bring it to the people God created. As Kate says,

> I truly believe that every girl should be a revolution. It's not often easy—actually, it rarely is—to stand against the crowd and to often stand alone. But we need more women (and individuals in general) to be a voice for this generation and other generations to come. We need heroes, revolutionaries, martyrs—anyone who is willing to take a stand, in whatever capacity, for the truth. The world has enough "lukewarm people"; we need more people who are on fire for the truth and who are willing to risk it all just to take a stand for something that matters.[10]

"Ask God to Break Your Heart for What Breaks His": Reggie Littlejohn

Once a high-powered attorney driven to make money, Yale graduate Reggie Littlejohn is the founder of Women's Rights Without Frontiers (WRWF), an organization dedicated to stopping forced abortion, forced sterilization, and female gendercide in China. Though she was raised in a Christian home, Reggie decided to become an atheist at the age of sixteen. It took many years before she turned to Christ, but there is no doubt she is on fire for Him now.

WRWF also runs the Save a Girl Campaign, where the organization sends field workers to the door of a woman who has been scheduled for an abortion or who is being pressured to abandon her already-born daughter: "We know her baby daughter is at risk, and we will literally go to her door and say, 'Do not abort. Do not abandon your baby just because she's a girl. She's a precious daughter, and we will give you monthly support for a year to empower you to keep your daughter.' We've had a tremendous success rate, and we've saved probably over 150 babies from abortion or abandonment or just crushing poverty."[11]

Reggie believes that women around the world are neighbors and that we are called to love each other as we love ourselves: "Jesus said to love your neighbor as yourself. And who are our neighbors in the twenty-first century? Our neighbors, I would say, are every single person that we know about, especially since you can now touch people on the other side of the world. I know about these women who are being forcibly aborted and abandoned. I know about women who are being pressured into selectively aborting their daughters just because they are girls. And because I know about them, they become my neighbors."[12] She also believes that whether a person is in the field or back home funding the cause, he or she is essential to the mission: "The donor somewhere who gave the money that enabled us to be at that door. And in God's economy, the donor saved that child."

After her marriage at the age of twenty-seven, Reggie suffered two excruciating miscarriages. Although she acknowledges that her experience is not the same as the women in China who are strapped down to a table and forced to have an abortion, she understands the pain of losing a desperately wanted child.

After her first miscarriage, Reggie asked her mother, "Why would God allow me to become pregnant with a baby who would be loved and cared for wonderfully in this world—and then take that baby away?" Her mother replied, "We will never know the answer to that question, but God does everything for a purpose. And I believe if you offer your suffering up to Him, He will use it."[13]

During a health crisis in her own life, Reggie prayed what she called a "dangerous prayer." As she suffered through bilateral mastectomies and the MRSA super bug—which left her with little hair, lying flat on her back, and disabled for five years—Reggie prayed, "God, break my heart for whatever is breaking Yours." She continues:

> And He broke my heart for the women and the babies of China, and I've dedicated my life to that issue. Now, that's not the only thing that breaks His heart. There are many things that break His heart, and every one of us is called to redemptive work . . .
>
> [Jesus is] our example, so people cannot simply throw up their hands and say, "There's just so much going on in the world," and then they end up doing nothing.
>
> I would advise them to ask God to break their hearts for whatever breaks His heart—to ask Him to reveal to them what He would have them do and to open doors for them to do it.

> It could be as simple as helping somebody in your family, or it could be running some kind of worldwide organization, or anything in between. But everybody's got to do something. And if you don't have time to do something—like let's just say that something really breaks your heart and you legitimately don't have time to do something—then you can always pray for that cause or pray for whatever organization is doing the work. And that is a spiritual sacrifice.
>
> You can also give money. Our time is limited, but we can give money to other people who are on the front lines in organizations that are directing issues that people care about.[14]

In addition to her compassion and grief for the women and babies of China, two things motivate Reggie: "One was my freedom as a woman and second, my sense of injustice that this was happening to other women who are sharing the earth with me at this very moment. I just couldn't believe it that this was happening in the twentieth century, now the twenty-first century. And I was walking around enjoying my freedoms as an American when there were these women who were [having forced abortions] and [being] forcibly sterilized in China."[15]

WRWF was born when Reggie heard the calling of God and simply couldn't stand the injustice to her fellow women any longer. While WRWF is not a Christian organization, Reggie runs it with the heart of a follower of Christ, desperately desiring to bring God's justice in her advocacy work for these oppressed women and girls.

Rescued to Rescue Others: Christina Marie Bennett

Christina Bennett is an inspiring millennial woman of strength who fills others with the hope that change truly is possible. Christina lives up to her name—follower of Christ—as she desperately seeks ways to make Jesus known through hopeful, passionate, and truthful conversations. Christina is particularly committed to prayer, peaceful activism, and speaking out for children in the womb. She currently works as a blogger and for a nonprofit organization that serves pregnant women in crisis and their families. Perhaps most inspiring of all is Christina's personal history. As a baby in her mother's womb, Christina was rescued through one very brave conversation.

Facing what seemed like overwhelming circumstances, her mother had scheduled an abortion. She was waiting in the hallway of Mt. Sinai Hospital in Hartford, Connecticut, and had just met with a counselor who had assured her that she was making the right choice. That's when an African American janitor noticed her crying and asked, "Do you want to have this baby?" Christina tells the rest of her story: "When my mother said yes, the janitor replied, 'God will give you the strength.' After the janitor's encouragement, the doctor called my mother into his office. She told him she changed her mind and wanted to leave. To her dismay, the doctor demanded she stay, insisting it was too late and telling her she had to go through with the abortion. With strength from above, my mom walked out."

Christina knows that simple conservations can save lives, shift minds, and change outcomes: "Conversations can reveal our identities and propel us into our destinies," she notes. "We must never underestimate the power of a conversation."[16]

Christina's inspiration for working for justice for all women comes from a very special foundation: the women in her own family. She says, "I grew up in a family of strong women. . . . The example my family set for me gave me an understanding that women were important. Seeing the way my aunts and mother were mistreated also gave me a desire to see women receive justice. I want to take a stand against the evils I see inflicted on women in society. I want to be a defender of women and a cheerleader for them."[17] Christina explains how a person can—and indeed should—be both pro-life and pro-women:

> My pro-life stance springs from the belief that all people are created equal and should therefore be given equal rights. The preborn child in the womb has just as much value and importance as any other human being. Preborn baby girls deserve protection just as every woman does. As an African American woman, I realize if I lived in a different time, I would have been seen as three-fifths of a person or as property.
>
> Regardless of what the law of man would have said about me, I would in God's eyes be a human worthy of dignity. The same applies to the preborn. To be pro-woman, you should be first pro-life, because every woman is first a fragile child. A child must be nurtured, protected, and cared for in order for them to grow into a beautiful and strong woman.
>
> Women face a number of serious, complicated issues in this day. To be pro-women means we must care about the needs of women and act to assist them. I desire to see women prospering and living out their God-given purpose. I want to see women flourishing in their careers, callings, personal lives, and in their relationships.
>
> I fight for the ending of abortion because I believe abortion hinders a woman's potential. Abortion has wounded many mothers and stolen the destiny of countless children. The fight for women's rights and equality begins when we stand up for our smallest sisters.

Christina pictures true justice for women across the globe as a broad, healing, empowering (and attainable) dream:

> I think true justice around the globe will take on many forms. It will include better education for women. I spent a few months in Mozambique as part of a ministry that helped build schools for children who lacked education. Learning is a key part of women's development and freedom.
>
> I also believe justice will be seen as women are rescued from sex slavery, work labor camps, and imprisonment for religious purposes.
>
> The outlawing of abortion will bring justice to women because abortion destroys the life of a child and has brought great suffering to many women. Women receiving better health care, greater support in pregnancy, and adequate maternity leave is vital. As a client services manager at a pregnancy center, I see many women who lack housing, are in abusive relationships, and stuck in low paying jobs. These are worldwide problems that must be addressed.
>
> In addition, too many women are voiceless, silenced by fear. . . . I want to see communities change so women are empowered to live out their dreams and raise their voices.

Christina's advice for millennial Christians who desire to get involved in women's justice issues is just like her—bold, timely, and beautiful:

> Don't get stuck in one version of what feminism looks like. The early American feminists fought against slavery and called for its abolition. In the 1970s, feminism

became synonymous with abortion rights and birth control. I believe feminism is different than that.

Feminism is fighting for the needs and rights of women. A true feminist is a friend of women. I urge women to find a version of feminism that fights for all women—from the preborn to the elderly.

When it comes to justice issues, I believe we are called to different battlegrounds. Some women will spend their lives focused on improving working conditions, while others will instruct moms how to grow in their domestic skills. Some women will travel to foreign lands to care for orphans and widows, while others will spend their lives caring solely for their family. It's important that we don't compare our roles or feel one calling or career choice is better than the other. As women, we must get involved with the justice issues we are called to and support other women as they live out their individual, God-given destinies.

In 2005, I left my home to move to Washington, DC, to take a stand against legalized abortion in America. We all must be willing to leave our comfort zones and follow the call for God's justice wherever it leads us. We must act, and act now, with passion, kindness, and strength.[18]

Doing Justice

For specific action points, see Chapter Eleven. In this chapter, you'll also learn how to develop your own plan to do justice in this area. More resources, ideas, and information can be found at my Facebook page, https://www.facebook.com/KristiBurtonBrown/.

CHAPTER SEVEN

On Every Street Corner

Homelessness, Poverty, and the Worldwide Refugee Situation

There are many in the world who are dying for a piece of bread, but there are many more dying for a little love.
—Mother Teresa

Poverty, homelessness, and the international refugee situation combine to form one of the most diverse issues we face. Many causes are discussed, solutions presented, and effects contemplated, and there are a variety of proposed solutions.

Internationally, the World Bank considers a person impoverished if he or she lives on $1.25 or less a day. In the United States, we are considered impoverished if we live on less than $16.32 a day. The difference seems staggering; however, we must remember that the cost of living in the United States is much higher than in other countries.

1,000 Days, a global nonprofit that works to keep women and their children healthy during the one thousand days between conception and the child's second birthday, explains the devastating effects of poverty early in a child's life—specifically in developing nations. According to this organization, "evidence shows that the right nutrition during the 1,000 day window can save more than one million lives each year," and that "leading scientists, economists and health experts agree that improving nutrition during the critical 1,000 day window is one of the best investments we can make to achieve lasting progress in global health and development."[1] Projects like Compassion International's Child Survival Program are designed to change the bleak statistics and give each child a chance at far more than survival.

According to the World Bank, the three most impoverished areas of the world are (1) sub-Saharan Africa, (2) fragile and conflict-affected regions, and (3) South Asia.[2] In these three areas, anywhere from 24.5 to 46.8 percent of the population is impoverished. Many live in refugee camps.

Such a wide range of people groups are affected by poverty, it would be impossible to adequately cover them all in one chapter. For instance, we will barely touch on the situation of orphans, and yet their needs are staggering. Because the plight and poverty of refugees is usually caused by violence or persecution, we will specifically discuss refugees in the following section. The World Bank lists them as among the most impoverished people in the world. We cannot discuss poverty without discussing refugees.

Next, we will flesh out our discussion on poverty in general by analyzing three main causes. There are certainly additional causes that are particular to unique situations. Some are more prevalent in the United States and Western nations, while others are more prevalent in developing or war-torn countries.

Whether we are talking about refugees, an impoverished inner-city family, or our newly homeless coworker, let's pray together for wisdom on how we can bring justice to those who are crying out for hope and a new life. As we pray, let's consider real action. James 2:15–16 clearly talks about the Christ-follower serving the poor: "Suppose a brother or a sister is without clothes and daily food. If one of you says to them, 'Go in peace; keep warm and well fed,' but does nothing about their physical needs, what good is it?"

The International Plight of Refugees

The U.N. reports that "every minute eight people leave everything behind to escape war, persecution or terror."[3] Statistics compiled through the end of 2011 show that "an estimated 43.3 million people worldwide were forcibly displaced due to conflict and persecution. [They included 15.2 million refugees.] Among refugees and people in refugee-like situations, children constituted 46 percent of the population."[4]

Top Ten Countries of Origin for Refugees, 2013[5]

Country	Number of refugees
Afghanistan	2,556,600
Syrian Arab Republic (Syria)	2,468,400
Somalia	1,121,700
Sudan	649,300
Democratic Republic of Congo	499,500
Myanmar (previously Burma)	479,600
Iraq	401,400
Colombia	396,600
Vietnam	314,100
Eritrea (located in the Horn of Africa)	308,000

The United States is the top country in the world in which refugees resettle. In 2013, we took in 66,200 refugees—nearly five times the number that the second country, Australia, took in.[6] Yet, according to the U.N., "resettlement needs continued to exceed the number of places available by a ratio of twelve to one." This is one reason American Christians need to find a real solution to illegal immigration in our country. Do our policies prevent legal immigrants—like refugees who have been waiting for years and are attempting to enter through the proper channels—from escaping horrific situations?

Millions of refugees live in camps as they flee violence, persecution, or certain death. Sometimes generations of families are born and grow up in these camps. The recent conflict in Syria involving the government, rebels, and ISIS has made Syria one of the most fled-from countries in the world at the time of this writing. In 2015, one of the refugee camps for Syrians in Jordan became the third largest "city" in that nation.

Kenya has hosted a massive complex of five refugee camps (including the largest in the world) for years. More than six hundred thousand people live in the camps, and many were born and raised there and have never been able to leave. In May 2016, Kenya announced it would be closing all the camps. Where will the refugees go?

On World Refugee Day in 2014, *International Business Times* wrote about the world's largest refugee camps, detailing some of the rampant problems and humanitarian disasters inherent in them:

- Lack of access to latrines and unsanitary conditions
- High death rate among children under the age of five
  - In one Ethiopian camp, "an average of ten children under the age of five die every day."
- Malnutrition
- Cholera outbreaks
- Poor hygiene
  - In a camp in Gaza Strip, "90% of the water is unfit for human consumption."
- Inadequate shelters
- Gender-based violence

- In one of the best camps, located in Jordan, women and girls are still disproportionately in danger and "at high risk of violence." They reported that they "felt unsafe using the toilets and communal kitchens," and some "refused to leave the tents they shared with their families."[7]

When we discuss the incredible predicament of refugees, we have not even begun to cover the difficult circumstances facing internally displaced persons (IDPs). An IDP is a person who, usually because of a natural disaster, has had to flee his or her home but still remains in his or her own country.[8] By end of 2013, an incredible 33.3 million IDPs were reported around the world—"the highest ever recorded."[9] These people also need compassionate and practical aid.

Refugees and IDPs also bring up the issue of children who are orphaned by war, violence, and natural disasters. Organizations like Kinship United work with local churches and create rescue centers to "rebuild loving families for orphans" in their community and provide them with proper care and a future.[10]

Three Common Causes of Poverty—Other than War, Violence, and Natural Disasters

The roots of poverty run deep. It is caused by a variety of issues that would be impossible to fully flesh out in one chapter. Sometimes poverty is brought on by life choices; other times, poverty comes to people by circumstances beyond their control. Regardless of the *whys* of poverty, Scripture instructs us to "defend the rights of the poor and needy"[11] and to "not exploit the poor because they are poor."[12] Understanding some common causes of poverty will help us identify the rights and needs of those in poverty and aid us in coming to solutions together.

The Connections among Divorce, Promiscuity, Fatherlessness, and Child Poverty in the United States

Evidence-based statistics show that marriage is "America's greatest weapon against child poverty" and that "being raised in a married family reduced a child's probability of living in poverty by about 82 percent."[13] Data from the U.S. Census Bureau proves that "single-parent families are significantly more likely to fall into poverty than are married-couple families."[14] Ron Haskins, senior fellow at the Brookings Institution, asserts that "there is widespread agreement among social scientists that marriage reduces poverty and helps make both children and adults happier and healthier."[15]

Children in single-parent families are reportedly "more likely to have emotional and behavioral problems; be physically abused; smoke, drink, and use drugs; be aggressive; engage in violent, delinquent, and criminal behavior; have poor school performance; be expelled from school; and drop out of high school."[16] Robert Rector, senior research fellow at the Heritage Foundation, further explains: "Comparing families of the same race and similar incomes, children from broken and single-parent homes are three times more likely to end up in jail by the time they reach age 30 than are children raised in intact married families. Compared with girls raised in similar married families, girls from single-parent homes are more than twice as likely to have a child without being married, thereby repeating the negative cycle for another generation."[17]

The great dangers to children and the risk of poverty in single-parent households is just one of many reasons Christians should protect traditional marriage. The fight for traditional marriage needs to expand until we are working to reverse our societal trend toward divorce and the prevalence of sex before marriage, especially among Christians. We should invest in work that strengthens families and keeps them together.

For those who doubt that sex before marriage effects the stability of a relationship, a recent study from a secular source—published in the American Psychological Association's *Journal of Family Psychology*—found that waiting until marriage to have sex makes for a better, more stable, and more enjoyable marriage, regardless of religion.[18] Of course, this makes sense, as God's principles apply to people whether they believe in Him or not.

A West Coast family law group published an informative blog post that details some of the effects of sexual activity before marriage and divorce on children and poverty:

- Living together prior to getting married can increase the chance of getting divorced by as much as 40 percent.
- In American families today, 43 percent of children are being raised without their fathers.
- Of children who live with a divorced parent, 28 percent live in a household with an income below the poverty line.[19]

For decades, study after study has confirmed that abstinence before marriage really is best for the health and stability of the marriage, and in connection, the health and welfare of any children involved. According to a 2002 study, "dissolution rates are substantially higher among those who initiate sexual activity before marriage [including living together before marriage]."[20] The research indicates that the rates of divorce are higher because the men and women involved have built their lives on "relatively unstable sexual relationships."

Glenn T. Stanton, director for Family Formation Studies at Focus on the Family and former consultant to the George W. Bush administration on fathers' involvement in the Head Start program, observes, "When we give ourselves away—and sex is a full giving of ourselves away physically, emotionally, spiritually—to someone outside the commitment and protection of marriage, it breaks down an important part of us, making our future relationships more unhealthy and difficult to sustain."[21]

Tom Tillapaugh, president of the StreetSchool Network, explains the disaster that has been caused by fatherless homes and homes where responsible choices are not modeled to children:

> The root of everything is fatherlessness. Even when I got into working against human trafficking, I found that out. I've had years where I've had no kids with a dad in the Denver Street School home. They don't come from broken homes that were once together; their home was never together. There is a direct correlation between the behavior of kids, troubles in life, and whether or not they have a father in their home. . . .
>
> Finding a thirteen-year-old girl having a baby with her own mother becoming a grandmother at twenty-eight is very, very common. There is no correlation in their mind between getting married and having babies. They have a daddy-sized hole in their hearts that a guy is trying to fill. She wants to be loved, somebody to care about her. So she gives in and gets pregnant. No discussion of even getting married. Poverty is a symptom and a by-product of these issues. Are there people who are together, married, doing everything right and still poor? Yes. But far fewer than people think. We're generations into this mess.[22]

In his 1999 memoir, *A Charge to Keep*, President George W. Bush wrote of the breakdown in the American family that concerned him as he ran for governor of Texas. He described the great need for personal responsibility. Because he believed strongly in giving a hand up to those in difficult situations, and because he wanted to help the next generation have a better chance at responsible, successful family lives, Bush proposed a solution in Texas that included limits on welfare benefits, job requirements for able-bodied recipients, school and training, child support, and drug-free contracts.[23]

Bush also believed that faith-based organizations and programs had high success rates and the ability to work well with people who needed help changing their lives. As Texas governor, he worked to "allow government agencies to contract or partner with faith-based organizations to deliver social services."[24] He made a point to inspire his agencies to find additional ways of working side by side with these often Christian organizations. Some were small, and some were large, but all, as Bush put it, were "leader[s] in the armies of compassion who are changing Texas, one heart, one soul, and one conscience at a time."[25]

He wrote very simply, "I believe in the power of faith to change lives." Followers of Christ must see the injustice being done to families—specifically, the innocent children involved—through personal irresponsibility, divorce, promiscuity, or abuse. We must come alongside people and offer a hand up. If marriage and a strong family unit are to be promoted as solutions to poverty, the church must lead by example, compassionately compelling others to follow.

The Lack of Expectations and the Need for Vision

Liz Murray, author of *Breaking Night: A Memoir of Forgiveness, Survival, and My Journey from Homeless to Harvard*, believes that it is important to set expectations for people as you love them. Born to cocaine-addicted parents, nearly starved as a child, damaged in the foster care system, and homeless by the age of fifteen, Liz found her mentor in high school when she decided, after her mother's death, that she had the opportunity for education, and she was going to pursue it.

Liz's life exemplifies the life of many experiencing poverty or homelessness. She had begun to perpetuate the cycle that was taught to her as a child. While she did not take drugs, she believed that survival was the highest goal in life. Finding food for that day or a place to sleep for that night was a great accomplishment. Liz's mentor, Perry, did not tell her that she was a victim, as so many had done before. Instead, while he told her that he was sorry for what had happened to her family, he saw her as a young girl who had great potential. He built up this potential by encouraging her, pushing her to do better, and teaching her that she should give back and volunteer—even while she was still struggling herself.

Liz credits Perry with setting the right expectations that recognized her potential and enabled her to see that so much more was possible, despite the setbacks most saw and the pity most afforded her. Perry revealed that there were standards she could live up to. Today, Liz is a researcher, author, speaker, and mom studying for her master's degree at Harvard.

While the Bible certainly does not give us a script to speak to those in poverty, and while there is certainly not a one-size-fits-all approach, Liz's story is worth considering. As Christ-followers, we can help encourage, inspire, and propel others forward. It is hope that breeds expectations and vision.

Pastor Gene Roncone explains, "The best way to fight poverty isn't by creating the expectation of entitlement. It's by transforming the human spirit. Our greatest challenge isn't poverty, food, or economic disparity. Our challenge is nurturing the self-worth in people that make them choose an honest $25,000 a year living over a $50,000 a year life of drugs and crime."[26] Of course, Pastor Gene insists that true change and real vision is only possible when evangelism is included in our compassion and justice. Without Christ, all else falls flat.

The Need for Economic Inclusion

Economic inclusion and the direct meeting of material needs for the poor provide a twofold opportunity. First, it provides the opportunity to minister to our brothers and sisters in Christ who are experiencing financial difficulty or much worse. Compassion International has a multitude of projects that reach into Christian communities around the globe, providing them with material needs and the opportunity to better their own lives.

Second, ministering to the poor provides an opportunity to bring the needy to the Savior Who can meet the needs of their heart. Many in Compassion International's communities are not saved, but they come to Christ through the example of the Christians around them. Samaritan's Purse is another organization that is known for providing immediate material assistance in refugee camps or in the aftermaths of natural disasters. Yet, in addition to providing goods, they also share the gospel. Material assistance and economic inclusion must be combined with a verbal witness of Christ so the needy are not left in spiritual poverty, which is even worse than physical poverty.

When addressing international poverty, local people who intimately understand their own cultures will often have effective ideas and solutions that will inspire their communities to participate in economic inclusion. When organizations work directly with people on the ground to improve their lives, change happens. Partners International's Animal Bank program is a good example of one of these "on-the-ground" economic programs.

In *Harvest of Hope: Stories of Life-Changing Gifts*, Kay Marshall Strom describes the incredible organization of Partners International's Animal Bank in Cambodia.[27] The book is worth a read for anyone interested in combatting global poverty. The Animal Bank system demonstrates that the solutions to poverty are often found in recognizing and celebrating the poor as human beings who are capable of much more than we give them credit for. They, just like us, are created in the image of God, Who has blessed them with the talent, skill, and character to better their own lives when given the opportunity, wisdom, and resources. It would be unjust to forget that a person in poverty is just that—a *person*, a fellow human being, created by God with infinite value. We should view those in poverty as our partners and siblings in the Lord.

Jodi Visser, an advocate we met in Chapter Two, explains how success can be measured when we work to help those in poverty:

> Every successful nonprofit geared at helping the poor that I have visited and spoken with will guarantee to you that to help the poor out of poverty is to *not* create financial or living dependencies on others, but instead to help people by giving them the dignity to recognize their own wonderful gifts and talents to provide for themselves by way of healthy discipline, education, and the freedom to work hard and smart—and therefore, be a healthy part of a community. Everyone has value and gifts to offer; we should always remember that and work to help bring out the best in people. That's what helping the poor is really about.
>
> We really should stop creating unhealthy dependencies, especially when developing countries are trying very hard to do the opposite to get *out* of poverty.[28]

Real-Life Justice Role Models

The following are the stories of some true social justice leaders who are seeking to make a difference.

Standing for Marriage and Real Fatherhood: Glenn T. Stanton

Glenn T. Stanton has been married for more than three decades and is the father of five children. Throughout his career, Glenn has focused on one thing: the building and cementing of the Christian family. His personal blog explains that he is a "contributing founder of the growing movement to recover marriage as a social resource in improving the well-being of children, women, men and communities."[29] Glenn has authored seven books and contributed to nine others, coauthored a film, and consulted for President George W. Bush's administration on education and fatherhood. He currently works as the director for Family Formation Studies at Focus on the Family and as a research fellow at the Institute of Marriage and Family Canada in Ottawa.

He graciously agreed to answer my questions[30] about poverty and the American family. He also recommended *The Family Project*, a twelve-part DVD small-group program put out by Focus on the Family (available at http://www.familyproject.com).

Q. What are the main ways Christians can promote marriage in our culture so that we convince people marriage is better than premarital sex, having children outside of marriage, and rampant divorce?

A. One is by us taking marriage seriously, honoring and fighting for our marriages, and coming together as a community for each other—to hold each person accountable and give help to each other with our marriages. Another is to have and build all this on a robust and spiritual theology of marriage. Not just Bible verses, or Bible lessons, or a systematic theology, but by understanding God and His story with us and how marriage fits into that. That is precisely what we do in our Family Project.

Q. Why do you think there is so much divorce among Christians?

A. Well, first of all, the divorce rate in the church is not the same as it is in the general population. This is as widely cited in the church as much as it's false. Christian couples who take their faith seriously and are active in their faith have a much lower rate of divorce. But most anyone would say that that rate is still high among Christians.

I think the reason is that we don't really know what we believe about marriage and why it matters. We are more like the world in thinking about marriage being about our own happiness and fulfillment.

Another thing that I think we could do in the church is make it a place where young couples can find and enter relationships with older couples who have been through thirty-plus years of marriage and can provide advice and encouragement in the midst of the troubles that *will* and *do* come to all couples. This is the primary thing that young people are looking for today: encouragement that marriage is a reasonable idea and real advice from real people on how to work it out. And the less perfect these older couples are, the better. No one wants to learn from the people who pretend they are perfect.

Q. Does divorce contribute to poverty and homelessness?

A. Oh, goodness, yes. Homelessness is not as common, but poverty is. Women who divorce—and women initiate the majority of divorces, curiously—tend to see a steep drop in overall household income. This comes in lowered earnings and increased monthly costs. This has been shown to be true through decades of good research.

Also, the divorced themselves are more likely to say divorce tends to simply trade one set of problems for another. This is part of why many judges increasingly say they are seeing couples who stood before them for a divorce return a few years later to get remarried. They realize that what they thought were insurmountable problems were not so bad, and in many ways, better than life after divorce.

Q. How do you motivate fathers to stay involved in their children's lives?

A. After divorce, we sadly see that most fathers want to stay involved in the lives of their children, but ongoing conflict with their mother can hinder that, often with the mother hindering this in different ways.

But for dads who just walk away, he can be motivated through the other men around him busting his chops a bit about walking out on his responsibility. It would be great if men would to this to and for each other. "Dude, get back in the game. No one else can play your position! Don't be a putz."

Q. What do you think justice for children in poverty would look like?

A. One of the biggest drivers of children in poverty in most of the world is fatherlessness. Kids who live with a married mother and father are almost never living in poverty. Kids who live with mom alone are nearly guaranteed to be. One leading scholar and child advocate said nearly all the increase in child poverty we have seen in the West today is due to the increase in single-parent homes.

So real justice for children in poverty—and not just a Band-Aid, however good-hearted it might be—is the marriage rate in a culture. No other factor impacts child poverty like this one does. No debate.

Q. Do you have any advice specifically for millennials who'd like to get involved in preventing poverty by promoting marriage?

A. Learn about the benefit of marriage sociologically. Lots of amazing data here.

And then become evangelists for it, increasing it for the benefit of children. Show marriage matters for very pragmatic human reasons, not just old-fashioned traditionalism or moralism, but for human thriving. It's a true, heavily consequential and countercultural message.

Saving Lives with Diapers and Formula: Quinn Anderson

In 2007, Quinn Anderson went on a trip to Juarez, Mexico, that altered the course of her life—and many others'—forever. Entering a world very unlike her own made Quinn see the basic necessities of life in a different light. She describes what she saw:

> **Diapers . . .**
> In Juarez—a ten-hour drive from Denver and a six-hour drive from Phoenix—many babies wear the same diaper for four or more days because the family can't afford new ones. A mom will go to the store with enough money for one diaper. The diapers are used and reused until they can no longer hold anything more, and the mom will go back to the store with just enough money to buy a new one. Cloth diapers aren't an option because water is so scarce in Juarez. Our team in the clinic saw babies with horrible sores on their bottoms and the parents with no means to help them.
>
> **Formula . . .**
> Just a car drive away, many mothers are too malnourished to breastfeed, and babies are dying due to lack of proper nutrition. A mother's milk often dries up in the first 30 days after giving birth. Up to 25 percent of the babies in Kilometer 30 (an area in Juarez) don't live

> longer than six months. It's extremely common for parents to not name their babies until after six months because of the terribly high infant mortality rate. Formula is literally life itself to these people.
>
> My babies did not go without food. My babies didn't go more than a few hours without a clean diaper, much less days. My babies were named before they were even born. I feel compelled and privileged to do anything I can to help these incredible people.[31]

For years now, Quinn and her relatively small team at Babies of Juarez have been traveling down to Juarez to deliver donated diapers and formula. When they can, they also bring blankets and coats, as the winters in Juarez are harsher than many realize. They work with local pastors and churches so that the supplies are passed out to the families who need them most.

Serving the poor in Mexico is a perfect fit for Quinn's family. Not only have they fallen in love with the Mexican people; they are also close enough to call them neighbors—people they simply can't ignore and allow to suffer. Quinn has involved her children in this justice work, providing an excellent example of how to teach our children to serve and give unselfishly.

Quinn shares her amazing perspective on the justice involved in giving to these poor families: "I think we've been given an awful lot, materially speaking, in this country, and I strongly believe we should have a love for sharing what we've been given. The people in the *colonias* have more material needs than I do, but in return, they share so much more with me. They have such contented spirits and gratitude for everything. They really depend on God in ways I often get wrong. So yes, I think it's right and good to give what we have to those in need. But it's far from one-sided."[32]

Quinn sees firsthand the difference that meeting basic needs makes: "The families we serve have the most basic needs. Food, shelter, water, education—and Jesus. Most of them are well-loved, but families struggle to find work. When you can't work, it's hard to meet the most basic of needs. When we get a chance to help with just one of these areas, it frees up their limited resources to focus on the others. It has an amazing trickle-down effect."

Quinn also believes that there is more than enough justice work to go around; we simply have to ask and be willing to obey: "If you ask God for a place to serve, He will give you one. Plain and simple. He created us to show our faith through deeds—and He's already planned those jobs. God forbid we miss the opportunity because we're too wrapped up in our own lives. It's a constant struggle for us, I think. It's so easy in our culture to get distracted and wrapped up in what isn't really important. Ask God to point you to your jobs and he will."

While Quinn says that she's "not one for giving advice," I appreciated her willingness to share how she discovered what she calls her "life's work." Her experience serves as a real, tangible example for millennials who are ready to put their faith in action:

> I was willing to get out of my comfort zone and put myself in a position where God could really speak to me. And when He told me after our first trip to Juarez that He wanted me to start collecting diapers and formula, I said yes. That's really it. He told me what He had for me to do; I said OK. He's been so faithful to honor that obedience, and He continues to give us the privilege of watching Him feed the babies and give people homes. It's been the craziest ride, and I wouldn't give it up for anything in the world.
>
> Be willing to get uncomfortable and get involved.[33]

Willing to Follow Where He Leads:
Brandon and Heather Culp

Brandon and Heather work with Casas por Cristo—Houses for Christ—as volunteers. But for eight years, Brandon was on staff in Mexico and in Guatemala, "trying to meet the peoples' most basic needs while getting to share the love of Christ with them."[34] For several years, Brandon directed operations in Guatemala and then in Juarez, and Heather faithfully worked beside him. Whether on staff or as volunteers, "getting to share" is exactly how Brandon and Heather view their work. It is a gift to them, a precious opportunity, and a way to be the hands and feet of compassion and justice to people who are much loved by our Savior.

Heather explained what inspired her to serve this particular group of people. When she married Brandon, he had already been working with Casas for years:

> On our first anniversary, Casas began its first expansion to another country. Brandon was asked to be a part of that, and for two weeks, he went to Guatemala to build homes for people in need.
>
> When he came back, it was obvious that he loved everything about it. About a year later, I was able to go on a trip with him to Guatemala. By the end of the week, both of us had begun to feel that we could serve full time there. Our hearts were drawn to the people and culture here in a way we hadn't felt before. The majority of the people don't have adequate homes, clean water, enough food for two meals a day, or any sort of health care. We felt that by moving here to Guatemala full time, we would be able to help improve some of these problems.

Just like the needs Quinn Anderson sees in Juarez, the needs of the people Brandon and Heather serve in Guatemala are very basic:

> The biggest need that we see is housing. Through Casas por Cristo, we work with the local pastors to find people in the communities who are in desperate need of a home. Our pastors present their applications, and groups from the United States come down and build the homes.
>
> After a year of being here, we began to notice a trend. Many families would still have problems with their health that they could not afford to treat. When we looked into the causes, the biggest issue was that they didn't have access to clean water. Recently, we have begun working with a company down here that manufactures water filters that will last a family for three years. We have begun working to provide one of these to every family that receives a home.

Heather has a twofold picture of justice: first, it's focused on our relationship with and reflection of Christ; and second, it's focused on real solutions for the people we serve. She and Brandon exemplify a willingness to search out the needs for justice, discover real solutions, and find the best ways to implement them:

> In Micah 6:8 it says, "And what does the Lord require of you? To act justly and to love mercy and to walk humbly with your God." It is hard to know exactly what justice would look like, but the best way I have found to answer that is to do my best to be a reflection of Christ wherever I am.
>
> It is difficult here, because I do not believe that throwing money on a problem will help it. The people here are some of the most impoverished people I have

> met, but they don't need money. They need a way to provide for themselves. I began a fair-trade store down here with the goal of helping teach a trade. We have taught people how to sew many different things and how to make all sorts of bracelets. Our neighbors who struggle with providing food for their family of eleven—we taught [them] to plant seeds and grow their own food.
>
> I think this is the beginning of what justice looks like—helping the people around you in a way that isn't just a short fix but will be able to help them for the rest of their lives.

Heather's advice to millennials is simple and bold:

> My advice is to take a leap. Everyone is not called to be serving in another country, but everyone is called to love. Sometimes we are going to be in uncomfortable places, but Christ didn't tell us that following Him would be easy. I believe that God placed these people on my heart for a reason. We could have stayed serving in Mexico, and I don't believe it would have been wrong, but I also don't believe it was His best. When we moved here to Guatemala, it was the hardest, yet most rewarding thing I have ever done.[35]

Indeed. There is no better, safer, or more rewarding place for us than the center of the will of God.

Doing Justice

For specific action points, see Chapter Eleven. In this chapter, you'll also learn how to develop your own plan to do justice in this area. More resources, ideas, and information can be found at my Facebook page, https://www.facebook.com/KristiBurtonBrown/.

CHAPTER EIGHT

Appointed to Die

Advocating for People with Disabilities in a Society That Discards

Love isn't a state of perfect caring. It is an active noun like struggle. To love someone is to strive to accept that person exactly the way he or she is, right here and now.
—Mister Rogers

God Himself will be with them.
—Revelation 21:3

Many different issues are involved in advocating for people with disabilities. Babies with disabilities are recommended for abortion at astounding rates.[1] For example, Dr. Peter McParland, an OB-GYN, explains: "In Britain, 90% of babies with Down's Syndrome are aborted before birth. In Iceland, every single baby, 100% of all those diagnosed with Down's Syndrome, are aborted. There hasn't been a baby with Down's Syndrome born in Iceland in the past five years."[2] Children born with deformities or disabilities are often abandoned and left to die or placed in orphanages that abuse them or are unable to meet their medical needs. All too often, schools cannot meet the needs of children with disabilities, and some workplaces do not have the appropriate accommodations—though improvements have been made in both of these areas.

There is also the lack of care provided to the elderly and those diagnosed with terminal illnesses. Despite the glowing news stories on euthanasia and assisted suicide, these people often do not "choose" to die—they are pressured into it, often after becoming disabled, or it is forced on them against their will when they can no longer care for themselves. They are made to feel that they have nothing left to offer and that their pain makes them useless. Where hope could be offered and needs could be met, a Nazi-esque "final solution" is suggested and implemented.

An entire book could be dedicated to these issues, but in this chapter, I will specifically address prenatal diagnoses and children with disabilities.

Prenatal Diagnoses

In the United States, there is a culture of death surrounding the diagnosis of disabilities—specifically when this diagnosis is made prenatally. Mark Bradford, president of the Jérôme Lejeune Foundation USA, writes, "To paraphrase the recently deceased disabilities rights activist, Dr. Adrienne Asch, the only thing prenatal diagnosis can provide is a first impression of who a child will be. Making such a radical decision as to end the life of a child based on a first impression is a most horrible and violent form of discrimination. It has no place in an American society that is committed to ending discrimination in any form."[3]

There are countless reports of parents receiving a prenatal diagnosis of disability or deformity, being presented with the worst-case scenario, and then being pressured into a rushed decision to abort. For example, 67 percent of babies who are prenatally diagnosed with Down syndrome in the United States are aborted.[4] Little—if any—hope is communicated, the positive facts and full range of treatment options are brushed over, and often, reevaluation is not encouraged. This is tragic in part because many parents who choose life, regardless of the pressure, have gone on to give birth to a perfectly healthy child or to a child whose disabilities are much less severe than initially predicted.

In December 2014, NBC reported that prenatal tests have a high failure rate, a fact that might lead to more women getting abortions: "Positive results can be wrong 50 percent or more of the time. And an investigation by the New England Center for Investigative Reporting published in the *Boston Globe* found that 'likely hundreds' of women are aborting fetuses based on this new generation of testing. One company reported a 6.2 percent abortion rate based on screening results alone—and without further testing, there is no way to know how many of those may have been due to a false positive."[5]

Nicole Steng, whose son Titus has spina bifida, shared her family's story:

> While they watched their eight-month-old son move his arms and head; while they saw his little heart beat quickly, the specialist diagnosed spina bifida and hydrocephalus, and put it all out there:
>
> He said it was the biggest lesion he had ever seen; that our son would probably never go to the bathroom on his own. He'd never walk, never talk. He said this based on a 30 second ultrasound. He said, "I will absolutely perform the abortion for you." I could see Titus' arms and head moving and his heart beating at the time the doctor said this. He was emphatic that Titus would be basically a vegetable and mentally retarded. And that it would be unfair to him for me to give birth.
>
> At that moment, Nicole and Steven realized that their role in Titus' life would be so much more than "parent." Their role was now "advocate" too. Without

> a word shared between them, both Nicole and Steven knew they would never accept abortion as an answer—no matter what the truth about Titus was.[6]

Despite the doctor's offer to abort Nicole's eight-month-old baby boy and his callous prognosis, Titus was born into a loving family where, despite his challenges with spina bifida, he has thrived. Today, he plays sports, talks very well, goes to school, and pops wheelies in his specialized chair—not at all the "vegetable" the doctor predicted.

Additionally, some issues and potential problems can be resolved while the baby is still in the womb, but this takes place after the stage of pregnancy when most abortions are performed.[7] This process cannot necessarily be predicted by doctors, but they still pressure parents to abort *now*. How many children have been aborted based on a misinformed or completely inaccurate diagnosis?

Molly, a young woman I grew up with, was given a prenatal diagnosis that turned out to be incorrect. Some of her son's health problems might have been resolved in the womb as she allowed her baby boy to live. During an ultrasound, Molly's son, Grayson, was initially diagnosed with hydrocephalus. Her doctor told her to consider an abortion, and a specialist gave this new mother the worst case scenario: "He could be brain dead. He might not live. He would have a deformed body."[8] Instead of giving in to the pressure and the medical advice that refused to give her son a chance, Molly says she "started to praise God for the life I had inside me."

Later, Molly was hit with another set of difficult news, as another test revealed that Grayson might have Down syndrome. She says, "I'll never forget when they told me Grayson had problems and to terminate my pregnancy, and today, he's 100% fine. Today, he's the brightest, healthiest, smartest little boy ever. I can't believe the doctor even thought it was the right thing to abort."[9]

While Molly's doctors were absolutely incorrect, she knows that giving life to her son was the right choice, no matter what the final result would have been.

Even if a devastating diagnosis proves completely true, children with disabilities and deformities deserve to live just as much as any other child. Our worth as human beings is not synonymous with our abilities, traits, or physical attributes. *TIME*'s prochoice writer Joe Klein covered the story of Isabella Santorum, the now eight-year-old daughter of presidential candidate and former U.S. senator Rick Santorum.[10] She was born with Trisomy 18, which is usually an early death sentence. In almost every case, the parents of these children are encouraged to abort. Klein wrote of being haunted by and grateful for the smiling photos he'd seen of Isabella with her family. They forced him to consider whether, as a society, "we've farmed out our responsibilities, especially for the disabled."[11]

Parents are sometimes still urged to abandon children who are born with cleft lips, club feet, spina bifida, Down syndrome, and the like. Not many years ago, Aiden Peterson was born with a bilateral cleft lip and palate at a hospital in Modesto, California. Instead of locating the proper supplies to feed Aiden at home, the hospital pediatrician recommended that the parents turn their new son over to the hospital. The plan was to put Aiden on pain medicine until he starved to death. His mother, Jodi, writes, "We couldn't believe they were giving Aidan this death sentence, but we would not abandon him. We could not imagine anything more heartbreaking than to have a helpless child left alone for the brief entirety of his life. Even if he had one day to live, he would spend that day being loved by us."[12]

Soon after the Petersons' decision, a lady who had herself been born with a cleft lip came to the hospital and gave the new family the supplies and support they would need to care for Aiden. For so many parents, help is out there. But they must first bravely choose life.

Children with Disabilities around the World

In September 2014, Human Rights Watch (HRW) reported that "nearly 30 percent of all children with disabilities in Russia live in state orphanages where they may face violence and neglect."[13] HRW released a ninety-three-page report—"Abandoned by the State: Violence, Neglect, and Isolation for Children with Disabilities in Russian Orphanages"—detailing the plight of these children. The specifics are disturbing, including descriptions of severe abuse and neglect. Children were tied to their beds and could not play or go outside, and many were not educated. HRW's report cited the "lack of adequate support and training for orphanage staff, as well as understaffing" as two root causes, along with the failures and inadequacies of multiple systems in the country. Additionally, HRW found that most of the children actually had a living parent, but trusted professionals had pushed many of the parents to give their children to the state, sometimes based on false information.[14]

Andrea Mazzarino, author of HRW's report, stated, "Many children with disabilities confined to 'lying down' rooms suffer stunning delays in their physical, emotional, and intellectual development. This is an avoidable tragedy if only all children with disabilities are given the proper nutrition, health care, and education that they have a right to."

Tragically, the plight of children with disabilities in Russia is replicated in many other nations. In China, such children languish in foster homes or orphanages, lacking basic health care to repair something as fixable as a cleft lip or a heart defect. While these children are often available for international adoption, the costs can be difficult, if not impossible, for willing families to meet.

In August 2015, CNN international correspondent Will Ripley wrote about JiaJia, a young boy whose lower body became paralyzed after a surgery to fix his spina bifida went wrong.[15] JiaJia has been waiting for a family for nine years; one already changed their minds. His new family is trying to raise the money needed to bring JiaJia—who wants to be a policeman—home. Ripley writes:

> The pain is evident in his voice as he explains why he wants a family.
>
> "If I have parents," he says, "I can live. I can have a life."
>
> Then the tears start streaming down his face. In seconds, I'm crying too. And so is every member of our crew. We sit together, crying in silence. For a brief moment, we understand JiaJia's pain.

Ripley states that there are more children just like JiaJia and that the majority of China's "unwanted children have disabilities." One research institute reported that the number of these often abandoned children grows by thirty to fifty thousand each year.[16] What's more, China's orphaned and abandoned children can no longer be adopted once they reach the age of fourteen.

Bulgaria has seen some of its worst human rights violations in its orphanages. In an orphanage in Pleven, it was discovered that the caretakers were neglecting and abusing children with disabilities. Adéye and Anthony Salem adopted one of the children from this orphanage. At fourteen years old, Hasya weighed just fourteen pounds. In February 2013, Rosa Monckton, who has been traveling to Bulgaria for years to try to alleviate the crisis there, wrote out the shocking details for *The Spectator*:

> I have been several times to Pleven, and carry memories that haunt me. I think particularly about the disabled children, locked away on a separate floor, many growing into the shape of their cots, and dying of starvation and neglect. These children are robbed of any chance of life. The stench of urine and faeces and rotting teeth is all-pervading. If evil has a smell, then this is it. Only

> 2 per cent of the babies in these institutions are actually orphans. The rest are abandoned due to poverty and parental neglect, and many simply because they are disabled. . . .
>
> Much of the damage to the children is due to a lack of stimulation and interaction. The children don't talk, because nobody has ever bothered to talk to them. They don't walk because they are never allowed out of their cots, and their muscles have wasted away.[17]

Monckton described a "Granny program" that was started after these atrocities were brought to light. Local women came every day to spend time with the children, and Monckton exclaimed over the difference that had already been made in a short time.

Children of every kind suffer in these types of orphanages and homes around the world. Yet children with disabilities are often the targets of the most grievous injustices. The work that must be done is staggering, but someone must take it on.

How can we inspire more people to adopt these children? How can we lower the costs? How can we change the orphanage, foster care, health care, and welfare systems in these nations? How can we advocate for the proper preparation and education of parents whose children are born with disabilities? How can we inspire entire nations to value and properly care for people with disabilities? How can we end China's one (now two) child policy, which has caused the current situation there? How can we transform cultures so that they value the orphan, the abandoned child, and the person with disabilities?

Real-Life Justice Role Models

The following are the stories of some true social justice leaders who are seeking to make a difference.

"No Greater Joy Mom": Adéye Salem

Years ago, Adéye and Anthony Salem noticed the abysmal state of care for people with disabilities in many nations around the globe. Often, these people live without adequate medical care, are abandoned by their families, and sometimes, are left to die without an ounce of love. The Salems have nine beautiful children. Six of them—five girls and one boy—were adopted internationally, and each of the six has disabilities or special needs, including Down syndrome, the inability to speak, and Hepatitis B. Their oldest child was discovered in an orphanage in Pleven, weighing in at just fourteen pounds at fourteen years old. She had been abandoned in a crib, forced to lie on her back, barely fed or changed for more than a decade.

Adéye and Anthony also recently adopted four embryos who had been frozen for ten years. These embryos had only a sliver of a chance at survival, but this couple chose to love them anyway and give them the chance at life they needed. These embryos had been created by a different couple at an in vitro fertilization clinic, and the biological parents had decided to give them up for adoption.

The Salems worked with Nightlight Christian Adoptions, a pioneer in embryo adoptions (also called snowflake adoptions). Three of the four embryos did not survive thawing, but one did. This tiny survivor was placed into Adéye's womb, but sadly, Adéye miscarried days later.

Despite the sad outcome of their snowflake adoptions, Adéye and Anthony remain convinced of two things. First, these babies deserved a chance at life, despite their unlikely chances of survival after being frozen for a decade. Second, every child needs love, despite disabilities, special needs, or quality or length of life. These four embryos were loved, and the Salems know they will see them in heaven one day.

Adéye has written about her personal transformation on her blog more than once, admitting that she once believed two children were her max[18] until Christ changed her "from the inside out."[19] Adéye and Anthony have taken ministry to people with special needs and disabilities to the most personal level possible: they chose to bring these children into their home, loving and caring for them daily. They provided these rejected children with a forever family, making all the difference in the world for these six little ones.

On her blog, Adéye tells her readers about other children with disabilities who need adoptive families. She pursues justice for them and has enabled multiple children to be adopted through her hard work, persuasive writing, passionate heart, and many prayers on their behalf. It's obvious that Adéye and Anthony view every child through the lens of love, firmly believing that every life created by God is a gift. Disabilities don't change the value of this gift or alter its preciousness.

Adéye sees the good that justice does for needy children, but she has also been blessed to see its work in her own life. She wrote the following about one of her adopted daughters:

> When God calls us to lay our lives down for the sake of one of His precious children, not only is it for the good of the child who needs us . . . but it's also for *our* good. . . .
>
> I am no longer the same person I was four years ago. God has used this one child on the planet to change me from the inside out. I see things differently because God knew that I needed this tiny girl. Truth be told, I needed Hailee so much more than she needed me. I have learned that God never calls His people to easy. No, He calls us to dig deep in His promises when we're holding

on for dear life. I have learned that there is so much joy indescribable in pressing in and embracing difficult.

I have learned that when we are faithful . . . so is He![20]

"Get off the Sofa": Brian Ivie and Pastor Lee Jong-rak

Brian Ivie is the millennial director of *The Drop Box*, a documentary featuring the work of South Korean pastor Lee Jong-rak. In the summer of 2015, *The Drop Box* became an inspiring call to Christians as it hit movie theatres nationwide, urging each of us to do what we can—in our own "small" or large ways—to save the lives around us.

Pastor Lee Jong-rak, moved to action in part by his own disabled son, created a literal drop box outside his church in 2009. In South Korea, babies born with a disability are often left to die, as their parents either do not want them or do not believe that they have the ability or the finances to adequately care for them. Pastor Lee allows parents to place babies in his drop box, which is warm enough for the babies to stay for a few minutes, until someone is notified that a new baby has come. Then Pastor Lee and his people give the baby a home in their orphanage or find a family, saving the baby's life.

Across the world, in the United States, young Brian Ivie had a desire for fame. When he saw Pastor Lee's story, he knew that he had to make a film about it. He was deeply touched by the work of this humble pastor, yet he also viewed making this film as a possible pathway to his own success.

Along the way, however, Brian's heart was transformed by the grace of God, and his motivations grew into something far more holy as he was personally brought to a saving knowledge of Jesus Christ. Brian told *World* magazine in March 2015, "What I didn't expect is that when I was going to go make a film about saving

Korean babies that God was going to save me."[21] Brian spoke of being incredibly touched by the "true love" of Pastor Lee. He marveled at the love that would compel this man, who "had drawn a line in the sand and said, 'No one dies here' . . . and said, 'I'm going to take care of you. I'm going to go after you, even though you may never know that I've done this for you, even though you may never know that you needed to be rescued.'"[22]

Brian told Religion News Service's Jonathan Merritt that he was not only saved during the making of *The Drop Box*; the project also "brought him a sense of purpose and freedom from struggles such as anger issues and pornography addiction."[23] He now sometimes writes an introduction to himself as simply, "Jesus Christ set me free."[24]

Brian was stunned when he first read about what Pastor Lee was doing, but he had no idea that one article would change his life forever:

> I read an article over breakfast . . . called "South Korean Pastor's Unwanted Flock." And it was all about this man in South Korea who had built a depository for disabled babies. I couldn't believe it. I was haunted by the image of this man holding a baby inside a box. At the same time, I was compelled.
>
> The images got into my bones the way the best stories did when I watched one movie per day in high school.
>
> It was like I was seeing real courage for the first time in my life. Courage displayed on a battlefield that I actually understood: a normal neighborhood. Not Gettysburg, not Iraq. Just someone's neighborhood. But the stakes were high. Life and death stuff. It was like this man had built a bunker for babies and was defending

> it with his life, saying, "No one dies here. Not in my town."[25]

Of course, as Brian later discovered, it was the love of the heavenly Father—displayed in Pastor Lee—that was resonating deep within:

> During the last interview for the film, I asked Pastor Lee a question that many have asked before. "Are you a hero?" I asked him with a cocky smile.
>
> Immediately, his head reared up, and he put his hand in the air as if to stop me from speaking.
>
> "All I am is because of God," he replied.
>
> So . . . that's what inspires me. When a man that the world applauds sticks his hand in the air and says, "I'm no hero. God saved me before I even wanted to save them."

Brian was further inspired that Christians—including his brand-new Christian self—should "get off the sofa and get into the battle":

> I think Pastor Lee is going after those that the world throws away. . . .
>
> In the Roman Empire, it was disabled babies, who were routinely "exposed" or left to die at the city gates until Christians started scooping them. In Nazi Germany, it was the Jews, homosexuals, and mentally ill, burned or gassed to death by the millions, and in twentieth-century America, it was the "feebleminded," sterilized by government order. And of course, all around the world today, it's the preborn. The problem for them is, they can't stand up for their own rights. Make no mistake though, they do have legs. They're just smaller.
>
> But what Christians need to know is that the history of our faith, no matter the blemishes and failures, is

> still chock-full of people fighting for the little guys in the hidden places. . . . Christians need to get off the sofa and get into the battle. That's where God is, anyway—in the battle, in the fog, in the thick of it.
>
> Remember, the cross wasn't just about perfect love; it was also about perfect justice. It was about destroying the devil and blowing a hole out the back of a grave.

Brian explains more about the efforts to build a rescue center for Pastor Lee and his family of babies:

> A good friend, John Stonestreet, once told me that the battle for life is much more about changing cultural consciousness and making the world look like "the home of Pastor Lee" than it is about law change. And honestly, I think that's why so many mothers bring their children to Pastor Lee. Because they see this man, who has loved the most "unlovable" people like his disabled son, and they think, "He won't hurt me. He won't shame me. He'll help."
>
> Right now, Pastor Lee's little three-story lean-to acts as a "rescue center" of sorts, but it's also become this beacon of hope for the abandoned and disabled in South Korea. So the basic idea behind the rescue center build is this: provide a larger and more equipped safe haven for mothers and children and make it the nation's headquarters for cultural change for the cause of life.[26]

After Brian responded to my interview, Kindred Image—Pastor Lee's nongovernmental organization (which Brian founded)—was able to raise enough money to move Pastor Lee into a new facility and also renovate Pastor Lee's original building into a maternity shelter so that more babies and mothers could be saved from abortion and abandonment.

As Brian explains, Pastor Lee and Kindred Image have a vision for transforming the culture around them as they save the lives of every "disposable baby" they can. Kindred Image describes its model:

> We want to put an end to abandonment but believe that this begins in the hearts of the people. Through story-based awareness, we work to change the cultural consciousness for the cause of life.
>
> While working to change the surrounding culture, we meet mothers in crisis and offer alternatives to abortion and abandonment in unsafe places. Kindred staff members serve at the drop box site on a daily basis.
>
> While engaging in crisis care, we also work to provide long-term solutions for single mothers and children left in the box. Through counseling, care packages, and adoption support, we are committed to holistic solutions.[27]

Brian offers advice for other Christian millennials who want to get involved in social justice issues:

> To be perfectly honest, I never wanted to be an activist. I never wanted to be involved with social justice. I wanted to be an entertainer. People like entertainers.
>
> But here's my simple advice. Are you ready? It's not that profound, but here goes: you can be both bold and loving.
>
> Some people scream at pregnant girls but don't really assist them. Other people are really nice, but they're afraid to speak the truth when it's difficult.
>
> But you can be both bold and loving.

> Do the work, don't complain, don't be a jerk, and try to understand why people have abortions. They have real reasons. So *please*, speak out against abortion, but *please* also open up your guest room to a mom in crisis.
>
> It's gonna take both.[28]

Just as Brian and Pastor Lee demonstrate, the only way to truly transform a culture and bring justice is to be personally involved (or to support those who are). Just because a person—like a pregnant mother seeking an abortion or parents seeking to abandon their child with disabilities—initially has a wrong response does not mean his or her needs are not real. With the right heart, we can meet the needs of parents and save their children.

Legal, political, and practical changes are all necessary. But at the core of the fight for justice is a change of heart. The human heart has to be transformed to practice justice instead of oppression, to reach for help instead of falling prey to fear, and to choose life instead of death. Christians also need a change of heart as we are moved to love people with the love of Christ, to speak the truth, and to meet the true needs of the oppressed and neglected with a heart of compassion.

Doing Justice

For specific action points, see Chapter Eleven. In this chapter, you'll also learn how to develop your own plan to do justice in this area. More resources, ideas, and information can be found at my Facebook page, https://www.facebook.com/KristiBurtonBrown/.

CHAPTER NINE

How Pastors and Christian Leaders Can Set the Example

This is no time for Christians in America to be silent! . . . The Word of God tells us to "Be on your guard; be courageous; be strong" (1 Cor. 16:13). We've got to take every opportunity to fearlessly defend our religious freedoms—and to point people to Almighty God and His Son Jesus Christ who is the only hope for our souls and this nation.

—Franklin Graham

I am not, nor will I ever be, a pastor. Yet there are a number of pastors and Christian leaders who have influenced me in my own justice work, and in this chapter, I will share their words of wisdom.

One of the most influential things a pastor has ever said to me was spoken after my high school graduation by my pastor, John Smith. He told me, "Kristi, you've started well. Make sure you finish well." On a number of occasions, Pastor John allowed me to speak to his small country congregation about the issue of justice dearest to my heart: the plight of the preborn child. He used his pulpit to call for justice in a number of ways and made it personal when he and his wife became foster parents.

If you are reading this as a pastor or a Christian leader, I hope you will consider what your colleagues have to say, and perhaps you, too, will take up the mantle of the justice issues of our day. If you already have, may you be inspired by the great host of Christian leaders who are leading God's people on to change the culture for Christ and bring His love and justice to the nations.

One thing is clear: we need your voice.

My husband, the son of an excellent pastor, reminded me that pastors are the only people who regularly have a captive audience of Christians—every single Sunday. Christian politicians or attorneys or activists don't have this. We typically have to rely on the media to get our message out—and whether we'll be accurately covered by the media is always a toss-up. Your occasional Christian blogger or writer has a regular audience, but it's rarely as predictable as the Sunday crowd pastors influence week after week.

As you read the following stories of pastors and Christian leaders who are working for justice in their own spheres of influence, consider how you can do the same. Perhaps there is a person in your congregation who could speak on justice issues. Maybe you will be willing to share your pulpit on occasion. You might already know a team of people who could get active.

You know your congregation. You know the people the Lord has entrusted to you. And you will know exactly how to inspire them to answer the biblical call to justice.

Politics Don't Scare Him: Franklin Graham

Franklin Graham—son of Billy Graham and founder of the worldwide Christian ministry Samaritan's Purse—illustrates the influence that a Christian leader can have when he is willing to speak out. Some Christian pastors and leaders believe that mixing theology and politics is dangerous, and they prefer not to bridge the gap. However, through the simple and effective use of his public

Facebook account, Franklin demonstrates that taking a public stand on the issues of our day is exactly what Christian leaders must do.

In early 2015, Kansas became the first state to pass a ban on dilation and evacuation (D&E) abortions. These abortions are performed in the second trimester of pregnancy and take the preborn baby apart, piece by piece. Kansas called the ban a "dismemberment" ban, since the procedure literally dismembers the babies inside their mothers' wombs. Here's what Franklin had to say:

> When some governors are backing up, Kansas Governor Sam Brownback is charging forward. I'm thankful for the strong moral convictions he and lawmakers in that state have shown by passing the nation's first law banning second trimester abortions. The "Unborn Child Protection from Dismemberment Abortion Act" ensures that babies cannot be torn apart limb by limb in the womb of their mother, a horrific and abominable procedure that has murdered millions of babies. Similar laws have been introduced in Missouri, Oklahoma, and South Carolina. Pray these states will act quickly to protect innocent life. Abortion is a bloody stain on the moral conscience of our nation, and I hope this legislation is a pivotal first step in putting a stop to the slaughter. "For You created my inmost being; You knit me together in my mother's womb." (Psalm 139:13)[1]

Instead of running from politics, Franklin has realized the influence he has been blessed with and uses it to speak out for justice. He has done this for other "political" issues that reach the national stage, including issues of religious freedom, marriage, and more. Through his position of leadership, Franklin does justice in many areas of life. His time might be committed to caring for the poor and needy around the world and to evangelizing, but he also carves out enough time to be involved with issues in the United States—even when they are considered "political."

He has also realized—and publicly shared—two essential things for Christian leaders to remember: (1) Christians and politics *must* go together, and (2) Jesus is still the answer, above everything else. He posted another compelling status on his Facebook page:

> America is in trouble. At 62 years of age, I've lived long enough to learn that neither the Democrats nor the Republicans can turn this country around; no political party or politician is the answer. The only hope for this country is Almighty God and His Son Jesus Christ. Next year I am planning to travel to all 50 states to conduct prayer rallies—we are calling this the Decision America Tour. I want to challenge Christians to boldly live out their faith and to pray for our nation and its leaders. I want to encourage Christians to get out and vote, and to cast their ballots for candidates who uphold biblical principles. I want to strongly urge Christians to run for public office at every level—local, state, and federal.[2]

A Skeptic Turned Hero of the Faith: Michael J. Norton

While not a pastor himself, Mike Norton is definitely a Christian leader and one of my mentors. A former senior attorney for Alliance Defending Freedom (ADF), Mike focused primarily on sanctity of life cases but has also been involved in religious freedom cases. One of ADF's chief goals is to inspire pastors to speak out about the political issues that Christians should care about. ADF enables pastors to boldly embrace the biblical calling to defend the oppressed and be a voice for true biblical justice.

Focused on sanctity of life, religious freedom (both at home and internationally), and marriage and the family, ADF has an entire website[3] dedicated to pastors and church leaders. With videos, sermons, a handbook, the annual Pulpit Freedom Sunday, and legal guidelines and assistance freely offered, ADF is ready to equip pastors to respond to the issues of our day.

But back to Mike, who now runs Colorado Freedom Institute in his spare time. His conversion story is a heart-rending one, as he became a follower of Christ on the day of his oldest son's funeral:

> I became a follower of Jesus on July 16, 1983, which was the funeral service of my oldest son, Jeff, who had just died of leukemia. During the course of his illness, he had become a Christian and a very active member of a church. He would encourage me to go, and I wouldn't. At the funeral service, his pastor made it a praise and worship service. He led all those present in the Sinner's Prayer, and I found myself joining in. A few days later, I thought, "What have I done?" and "What did it mean; what was the significance?" On a personal quest to understand my Christian faith, I consumed the Bible and Christian books recommended to me. I also started attending Bible classes and colleges. Over a thirteen- to fourteen-year period, I finished a masters of divinity at Denver Seminary.[4]

Dedicated to living his newly found faith, Mike wondered how he could best serve Jesus. For a time, he wondered if he should go into the ministry and become a pastor. But soon, Mike, already an accomplished attorney, realized that the ministry and the mission fields weren't the only places in which a person could serve Christ. Great work for Christ can be done in every sphere of life, and Mike knew that God had gifted him in "this law business," so he chose to "focus on helping people and on helping them find Jesus."

Mike shares his favorite moment of evangelism, which took place inside a jail with a client: "I shared Jesus with a Hispanic guy who needed an interpreter. When I looked up, he was crying, tears streaming down his face. He was accepting Jesus. The interpreter was crying too."

Whether it's through evangelism or through ensuring that the right to life, traditional marriage, and freedom of religion remain pillars of our society, Mike is committed to seeing his work through to the end: "It's sad to watch and see how we're spiraling ever downward into degradation and despair. We have to keep on keeping on in pressing the Lord's agenda."[5]

Serving His City: Gene Roncone

Sincerely passionate about serving his city, Pastor Gene Roncone, lead pastor at Highpoint Church in Aurora, Colorado, has inspired his congregation to bring justice to the people in their own neighborhoods. Pastor Gene also sits on the steering committee of Aurora's Gang Reduction Impact Program and the board of Aurora Warms the Night, an organization serving the homeless. He meets with other community leaders at Original Aurora Renewal, a group of residents and leaders interested in helping shape the community, to discuss how to "increase the quality of life and promote long term . . . health, safety and resilience in northwest Aurora."[6] Pastor Gene is part of the Key Community Response Team in Aurora as well—a group of volunteers and community leaders who respond for the city in times of civil disorder.

Deeply invested in his church and his city, Pastor Gene exemplifies a leader who is willing to get his hands dirty to serve the needs of his community. He's been willing to lead an initiative that provided new coats for at-risk children and families and has mobilized hundreds of local volunteers for various community outreaches. Pastor Gene has used his church to host community events that raise money for Aurora's homeless people. A second campus of Highpoint Church, located in the poorer areas of Aurora, has a food bank and a weekly faith-based children's program, where the kids are also served a hot breakfast. Pastor Gene shares what led to his involvement in justice work:

> For several years, I allowed success and an absence of comprehensive Bible reading to isolate me from God's heart for the poor and oppressed. I always spent twenty to twenty-five hours a week in the Word of God, but it was for sermon and teaching preparation. After a life crisis, I started reading ten chapters of the Bible a day in logical order. Being exposed to God's heart for the poor in every book of the Bible changed me forever.
>
> I started a two-year journey studying my city's greatest needs, working once a week from the worst neighborhood in town, interviewing community leaders and praying from a remote location [on the Colfax strip]. It was this process that resulted in my discovering where the church was needed most but present the least.

Pastor Gene shared five reasons he believes serving the poor and reaching out to the community are important issues for today's Christians:

1. All of humanity was created in the image of God. The Bible teaches us in Genesis 1:26–27 that all mankind were created in God's image. That means

all human life is sacred and endowed with dignity, value, uniqueness, and worth.

2. We have a Christian responsibility to be stewards of our earthly resources. The Bible teaches us that God gives us resources to bless others (1 Peter 4:10). If God has made us stewards of the world's resources, then we must use them to accomplish His will and purposes on earth.
3. Having experienced God's grace, we should want to share it. In both the Old and New Testaments we are taught that our own experience of grace should motivate us to be gracious to others. Jesus also said, "Shouldn't you have had mercy on your fellow servant just as I had on you?" (Matthew 18:33).
4. Jesus taught us to express faith in practical ways. The Bible encourages us to put action to our faith when it says, "faith by itself, if it is not accompanied by action, is dead" (James 2:17).
5. Christ expects each of us to reach our city's most needy places. Both Old and New Testaments teach us to serve our city and its most critical needs. God told Jeremiah this when he said, "Also, seek the peace and prosperity of the city to which I sent you. Pray to the Lord for it, because if it prospers, you too will prosper" (Jeremiah 29:7). Jesus also encouraged this when He said, "Go to the lost, confused people right here in the neighborhood. Tell them that the kingdom is here. Bring health to the sick. Raise the dead. Touch the untouchables. Kick out the demons. You have been treated generously, so live generously" (Matthew 10:5–8, The Message).

I asked Pastor Gene to comment on the main needs in communities across America. While he believed he was best equipped to answer about his own city, he did provide "common denominators" he's noticed as he travels:

- The church is absent in the most needy places of our cities. In most cases, there are more godless and liberal organizations with boots on the ground than the church.
- The church generally offers more opinions than resources, money and volunteers and partnerships and practical solutions.
- The church does little to no statistical or relational research on city needs and assumes their own needs are synonymous with the needs of their city.
- The church resents liberals so much that they distance themselves from issues associated with the left (compassion for the poor) even if God's Word calls them to these issues.
- The church is looking for a political party to be a "political home" when the fact of the matter is there is NO political party that can represent the totality of God's Word. We are Christians before we are anything else.

Our communities NEED the presence of the church. But the church must see themselves as needed and reconnect with their communities. There is a strategic and sacred role for the church in society. The church can:

1. Elevate the human spirit. The church can elevate the human spirit by appealing to the best, instead of the worst, that people can accomplish together.

2. Mobilize resources. The church can quickly mobilize people and resources to overcome difficult problems and meet complex needs.
3. Promote justice. The church can serve as a moral compass to help our communities navigate through the dark side of politics, materialism, power, selfishness and sin.
4. Meet unique needs. The church can fill gaps that government, education and political organizations aren't structured to fill.
5. Facilitate spiritual growth. The church can resource people's spiritual need for reconciliation by creating an environment for spiritual growth and discovery.[7]

Jesus as the Ultimate Justice Issue: Greg Stier

I first heard about Greg Stier in the little country church I grew up in. Even out there, his message was reaching us. High schoolers from my church would ride in a big van up to the big Dare 2 Share conferences in Denver, learn how to share the gospel, and come back on fire for Christ.

Greg has completely dedicated his life to spreading Jesus Christ, Who he knows is "the answer to every problem we are facing."[8] Amen! Thousands of young people have been reached by Greg's conferences, videos, and Bible studies over the years. Greg also has a website, where he provides youth leader tips, his life lessons, and even "rants."

There's a personal reason Greg is so focused on "gospel advancing." Years ago, when he was a lost child without a father, he was reached by a church that was involved in a dangerous inner-city mission. Greg shares, "I was a fatherless kid raised in a high-crime-rate area of my city when a church from the suburbs reached out and shared the good news of Jesus with my entire family. Suddenly,

I had a heavenly Father Who would never leave me or forsake me. That same church had a powerful youth ministry that literally reached hundreds of teenagers for Jesus in our city. The youth leaders inspired and equipped me to reach teenagers for Jesus, and I've been doing it ever since."[9]

The church that reached Greg must have known that, while people in the inner city have many needs, the deepest of them are met by Jesus Christ. Greg offers his thoughts on how to keep the gospel at the center of our work on human trafficking, poverty, foster care, abortion, and more:

> I use an old Charles Spurgeon term called "gospelize." When it comes to poverty, abortion, foster care, human trafficking, etc., we need to help young people gospelize their efforts. As Jesus said, what good is it if someone gains the whole world and loses their own soul? Taking care of human needs is only part of the equation. We must take care of their deeper, spiritual needs as well.
>
> For instance, Compassion International has done a phenomenal job of gospelizing their efforts. I've visited projects in El Salvador and Colombia and have been blown away by how central the gospel of Jesus Christ is to their humanitarian efforts. They take care of the whole child—physically, mentally, emotionally, and spiritually. They are gospelized from top to bottom. As a result, every graduate I've met from the Compassion Leadership [Development] Program has said that they are grateful for all that Compassion did for them—feeding them, educating them, taking care of their medical problems, etc. But what they are most grateful [for] is that Compassion introduced them to Jesus Christ.

> In the same way, if we don't seek to introduce those whom we are serving to Jesus, we are doing them a great injustice. After all, if we had the cure to cancer and those we were feeding had cancer, wouldn't we feed them *and* give them the cure? Of course we would! Well, we have the cure to something infinitely worse than cancer, and those who die without Jesus are headed somewhere infinitely worse than death. It would be a grave injustice to not share "the cure" with them. The cure is the gospel of Jesus Christ.

Greg explains what he thinks makes Christians shy away from evangelizing while doing social justice work. First, there's the "anemic theology that says we are to just preach the Gospel with our lives." Greg cites the Gospels and Acts, which detail how Jesus and His followers used their lives and their words to evangelize. "Like the two wings of a plane," Greg says, "both are necessary." Second, Greg shares that if Christians don't catch the urgency of the Gospel and people's need for salvation, and if they don't know how to explain it, this can keep them from evangelizing. Greg's ministry, Dare 2 Share, offers plenty of tools and resources for anyone who wants to learn how to effectively share the Gospel. Finally, Greg makes plain that a focus on money in social justice organizations can be a "roadblock that can keep Christians away from sharing the Gospel." He warns that we should be careful to not give up our essential "gospelized" mission to get government, grant, or other funding and points to the examples in *Mission Drift* for those who want more information.

From years of experience, Greg understands how we can motivate millennials to change this world for Christ:

> If we could frame sharing the message of Jesus as the ultimate social justice issue, I believe that we could

mobilize young people to truly change the world for Jesus. As they are providing those who are thirsty with drinkable water, they could also provide them the Living Water. As they are providing bread for the hungry, they could also provide them the Bread of Life. As they are building a house for the homeless, they could help build another one in heaven by sharing the good news of Jesus with them.

Also, unlike my generation, this generation of young people is not as familiar with the theology of hell. But Jesus spoke of it consistently. As a matter of fact, of the twelve times hell (*Gehenna* in the Greek) is mentioned in the New Testament, eleven are by Jesus himself. If young people could develop a heart that breaks for the lost, for the hell others are headed to, and for the "hell" many of them are going through, I believe they would be motivated to share the good news of Jesus and change the world on every level.[10]

Leading the Next Generation:
Quin Friberg and Seth Silvers

Quin (an apologist) and Seth (a leader in business ownership and orphan and youth ministry) are both millennial men who have taken up the mantle for their generation, striving to lead by example and bold words. One is married with two children; the other is newly engaged. One attended a public community college; the other the well-known Oral Roberts University. One was homeschooled through high school; the other went to different Christian schools. Together, Quin and Seth—who don't even know each other—illustrate that despite our backgrounds or our current circumstances, we can take hold of the plow and not look back. We are not constrained by "what happens to us." Instead, we are filled with the Holy Spirit, who leads us ever forward onto new, uncertain, and victorious ground.

Quin shares what inspires him and how he believes we can motivate our fellow millennials (and the younger generation) to actively change the world for Christ. He is convinced that our generation needs to hear the "hard doctrines" of Christianity and to face the reality of those suffering all around us:

> Over the past couple years, I started to see statistics that I'd read become a reality (to some degree) in my own life. Many of us have heard that 80 percent (different studies vary a bit) of Christian evangelicals lose their faith by the time they are finished with high school (or college), and it's really easy to keep that statistic impersonal in your mind until you see it happening to people you know.
>
> I think the best way to motivate people is to teach the whole truth; to not water down certain doctrines like hell because people don't like them. People need to know what's going on around the world and in our society. Many are so caught up in their own world that they don't know how bad other people are hurting. I wouldn't be motivated to help fix a problem if I didn't think that problem even existed.[11]

Seth shares his inspiration and his great hope for the decades ahead:

> Students have always captured my heart. Myself only being twenty-three, and seeing God move in my life in great ways at a young age, the potential of what God can do with students excites me. I love how young people are not fully aware of what they are capable of—or not

> capable of—and this naivety often causes young people to reach for the stars and actually touch them. I love the idea of seeing students lead the way in the social justice movement and becoming the example for the world for what it means to live a life of sacrifice. The need for justice around the world is obvious, but who is to help and how to help is always the question. I have been drawn to the idea of young people's destiny being rescued and revealed as they reach out to rescue the destiny of another in need around the world.[12]

He also explains the main needs he's seen:

> While working with students in voluntary slavery to consumerism and young people in involuntary slavery to global poverty, I see different needs. In America, I see needs for truth to be spoken, encouraged, and modeled. Young people in affluent countries need to see examples of people who are utilizing resources as a tool to serve, not a tool to satisfy. Students need to see that Jesus put them in a country with resources for a reason of restoring those in need.
>
> In poverty-stricken regions, I see a huge need for educational reform and economic encouragement. America has this new movement of entrepreneurs that is encouraging young people to truly pursue their dreams, and the economy is making it possible for many young people to start their own businesses and find their own means of financial sustainability. I believe this same entrepreneurial spirit needs to be spurred on in poor countries around the world.
>
> There are obvious needs such as health, food, and water that are necessary . . . we can't help people who

> don't get the chance to live. But once those living in such communities have their basic needs provided for, they need to be encouraged that they have potential, hope, and the means to live a life of purpose. The truest way to communicate this potential, hope, and purpose will always be through the message the gospel of Jesus Christ brings to people.[13]

Quin agrees that, in all our work for justice, we must strive to keep the gospel front and center:

> Our bodies have many ways of telling us that something is wrong, the most obvious of which is pain. If I were to go to the doctor, explain that I am in a lot of pain, and all the doctor does is give me pain killers to take the pain away, I am not going to be satisfied. When we go to the doctor, we want him to figure out the root cause of the pain. We are not just interested in taking away the symptoms, but in fixing the problem that is causing them.
>
> Social justice issues are symptoms of a bigger problem; they are evidence that something is wrong with our society (and the world as a whole) . . . which the Bible identifies as sin. I think it's a great thing to fight against these social injustices—it's something Christians should be actively engaged in—but at the same time, we can't just get rid of the symptoms. We need to address the cause. If the cause is sin, we have the prescription for it: salvation through Jesus Christ and a changed life that comes with true transformation by God. . . .
>
> How can we keep the gospel message central, though? There are many great Christian organizations that give people the opportunity to fight social injustices,

while at the same time preaching the gospel to those who need it. Many Christians I've met disagree with what I am about to say, but that's OK. I don't believe Christians should team up with Muslims, Mormons, Buddhists, etc., in order to solve social justice issues. Usually those partnerships focus solely on the symptoms and don't present anyone with the gospel. And if they do, oftentimes it will be the wrong gospel coming from a Muslim or a Mormon. Now there are obviously some exceptions to this rule. If I see someone drowning on a lake, and a Muslim yells for me to help get the guy out, I'm not going to ignore him and let the guy drown; that wouldn't be biblical. But whenever possible, I will work with believers in groups and organizations that understand the importance of the gospel being at the forefront when dealing with social justice issues.[14]

I asked both Quin and Seth to share their advice for fellow millennials who want to do justice in a world full of evil, suffering, and injustice:

Seth:

Christians need to not just share information on justice but be excited and willing to get involved. I think our role as Christians in a world filled with injustice is to live differently so others can live differently. Social justice can come off as intimidating, complicated, and too big to make a difference. Christians need to recognize and embrace that one of our primary purposes for existence is to restore the broken world around us, including the parts plagued with injustice. Once we embrace this as part of our identity, it becomes less intimidating and more attainable, because we recognize God will provide the wisdom, ability, and resources to be able to make the difference we were created to make.[15]

Quin:

The problem of suffering and evil has been used as evidence to "disprove" the God of the Bible. People ask me all the time why God lets bad things happen to people. Why does He allow suffering and pain? Where is He in the midst of everything? My view is the exact opposite (surprise!). I don't think any of this suffering and pain makes sense without God. Why is it that we have this idea of injustice? Most everyone agrees that there's something wrong with children starving in Africa and girls being trafficked around the world. But why do we all have this deep sense that these things are wrong? If there is no God, how do you define what is right and what is wrong? Why is it wrong to make money selling eleven-year-old girls?

The Bible tells us that God's law is written on our hearts, that we are made in His image, and that some things are wrong because they go against the nature and purpose of God.

How can we help millennials stay firm in their faith while working to fight social injustice? Equip them. The Bible gives us the answers to the questions we have; people sometimes just don't know what they are. We need to teach the truth without compromise. Christians need to understand what they believe and why they believe it, and sometimes that takes time. There are many great ministries and teachers that work to ground Christians in their faith and to prepare them for the questions others may ask—or that they may find them asking themselves. The Bible tells us to put on

> the whole armor of God, and oftentimes it seems like some Christians are running around naked on a battlefield with only the helmet of salvation. We need to be equipped and grounded in our faith if we are to effectively reach this world.[16]

Doing Justice

Pastor Robert Gelinas is heavily involved in orphan care ministries—specifically through the avenues of foster care and adoption. He offers great advice on dealing with the difficult or unpopular passages in Scripture that call a congregation to action and on how a pastor or spiritual leader can do justice in their own lives:

> Oftentimes, pastors . . . ignore those passages that clearly teach that we're supposed to care for orphans. And [there are] plenty of them. So I think the first thing a pastor can do is teach those passages. And teach them clearly—as clear as they teach any other passage in the Bible. I think that we need to do a good job of telling people what the myths are in foster care and adoption. Sometimes people don't get involved because they're carrying around these false ideas of what it might mean to get involved. And the pastor is the perfect one to stand up and say, "If you live out this verse in the Bible, here's what it will mean in your life." But all of that assumes that the pastor's involved . . . him or herself . . . that they somehow are caring for orphans. So maybe the number one thing a pastor has to do is say that orphan care is not optional for Christians. *It's as normal for us as prayer and reading our Bible, and we care for orphans.* The only question is, how do we care for orphans? (Italics added for emphasis)[17]

Amen. May our work on the justice issues that matter to the heart of Christ become as normal to us as prayer and Bible reading.

CHAPTER TEN

Can I Really Change Things?

The probability that we may fail in the struggle ought not to deter us from the support of a cause we believe to be just.
—Abraham Lincoln

Courage does not always roar. Sometimes courage is the quiet voice at the end of the day saying, "I will try again tomorrow."
—Mary Anne Radmacher

One of the Scriptures that first spoke to my heart about social justice is Proverbs 24:10–12:

If you faint in the day of adversity,
Your strength is small.
Deliver those who are drawn toward death,
And hold back those stumbling to the slaughter.
If you say, "Surely we did not know this,"
Does not He who weighs the hearts consider it?
He who keeps your soul, does He not know it?
And will He not render to each man according to his deeds?

This passage motivates me to do my part to speak up for those who have no voice, to work tirelessly to save more lives, to never give up. It doesn't guarantee success, but it does make my job clear. It reminds me that it's essential to focus more on my duty than on my results.

I was raised to believe that all people are valuable because we are all created in the image of God. It's another one of those down-home country values. It doesn't matter if we're white, black, brown, yellow, green, or purple (as my mom would say); it just matters that the Creator God made us and loves us.

My mom taught me that we all have a duty to stand up for the innocent—specifically those who can't speak for themselves. As a teenager, I pored over books written by Jews who'd survived the concentration camps in World War II and wished that I had lived back then so I could save more of them. I loved books about Sojourner Truth and others on the Underground Railroad, and I wished I had lived during those years so I could rescue slaves.

But my mom taught me something else important: God placed me in the exact time period in which He wanted me. There are people today who are innocent, are dying, and can't speak for themselves. *These* are the people God has called me to reach. He placed me in *this* specific time in history for a reason.

He placed you here too.

For me, this calling—this duty—is specifically to rescue the preborn children being aborted every day. When I was a teenager, I learned that in Denver, Colorado, one hundred babies die every week in just a single Planned Parenthood abortion clinic, and I thought, what are we doing to stop that, to save them?

And what about the thousands of children and women around the world caught in human trafficking? The slaves in Sudan and India, the ones captured by Boko Haram and ISIS? Christians who have no Bible in their own language to read and are tortured if they're found listening to a Christian radio broadcast? Starving children and families who have nothing to eat and have never heard the gospel? Unreached tribes? Abused children in the foster care system? International orphans? People dying of AIDS in field hospitals? Refugees living in deplorable camp conditions?

Our power is in our prayer (another one of my mom's quotes), and we should pray for these hurting, unreached souls every day. I'm a firm believer in prayer warriors and the power wielded by those who seek the throne room of God every day on behalf of others.

But we also need to get out there and do something to make a difference. Justice must be *done*, not only hoped for and prayed for.

There's no guarantee that everything will play out the way we hope. But we still can—indeed, we *must*—take action to be the answer to the prayers we pray. We certainly aren't going to change things if we don't choose to act.

The World Might Not Be the Size We Think

I clearly remember September 11, 2001; most people who lived through that day will always remember it. One of the memories that stands out most to me (other than my brothers and I being sentenced to our rooms for most of the day for arguing) is doing the dishes and hearing President Bush on TV, quoting Psalm 23:4 (KJV): "Though I walk through the valley of the shadow of death, Thou art with me."

But I also remember my dad sitting down with my brothers and me that night and saying that now it was up to us to change the world. If only every person would have that vision—it's up to *you*, it's up to *me*, it's up to us together to change the world. With the power of God living in us, we can do just that.

Changing the world doesn't require fame. It's not even necessarily about saving the lives of thousands or millions of people (though that would be great, and I'm definitely in favor of it). Changing the world is about making a difference *where we are today*.

So much of changing the world comes from being willing. It's about being willing to let God use us to touch the lives of everyone that comes across our paths. It's praying that the light, the truth, *and the love* of Jesus Christ will shine through us in such a way that every person who sees us will want Jesus too. It's about choosing a *them* and an *us* focus instead of a *me* focus. Each one of us really can change the world when we make daily decisions that honor God.

Be bold and ask God to show you how big your world is. Coming from the country like I do, it's easy to think that the world is huge: the sky never seems to end, the stars are bright and close, and the land stretches on forever. But we need to ask God the following questions:

- Do You want me to go out and reach the world way beyond my front door, my church, my school, my workplace, my community?
- Is my world bigger than I ever imagined? Or is my world much smaller?
- Am I forgetting the people right in front of my face?
- Am I forgetting the work You've already placed in my hands?
- Are the gifts You've already given me actually enough and worthy to be used in Your service?

Be ready for God's answer, whatever it is. Be willing to make your world bigger, and be willing to make it smaller. Be willing to see the world in front of you or the one beyond you. See the world that God sees.

Our view of people can easily become nearsighted or farsighted. If we're nearsighted, we focus on "me" or only on the people we love—those close to us, those who are easy to serve and get along with. We forget that there's a dying, suffering world out there God has called us to minister to.

If we're farsighted, we focus only on some "big" calling or vision. We begin to believe we're too important for the seemingly mundane, everyday tasks: "Me, serve food at a church event? Me, stay home with my children? Me, pick up the piece of trash on the floor at work? Me, do the dishes at home? No, no, no . . . God's called me to something *far* bigger than those little things."

We would do well to remember Luke 16:10–12 (ESV): "One who is faithful in a very little is also faithful in much." God is interested in *how* we complete the tasks He's given us for today. If we do them to the best of our ability, then God might be interested in expanding our world so we can faithfully reach more people for Him.

It's the Trying That Matters

It's cliché, right, to say that all we have to do is try. We want to believe we have more power than that. I want to believe that I have the power to save every single baby in the world. That I have the power to stop rampant rape and child marriage and the resulting fistulas that make women outcasts. That I have the power to keep every child under five alive, despite the lack of basic medical care in their countries. That I have the power to get every special needs child into a loving home.

If only I had such power.

But here's the thing: I don't. On our own, each of us is absolutely powerless. Yet we serve a God Who is more powerful than we can even conceive of. It's His power working through us, enabling us to save lives and make them better. It's His power giving us the words to evangelize and the resources to care.

Of course, there's always that one elephant in the room: If God is so powerful, why doesn't He just stop all these bad things from happening in the first place? Why don't His people always succeed?

Our hearts are drawn to the kind of world God originally created (the one we ruined through our sin), and that's the kind of world He's going to institute again one day in His eternal kingdom. An incredibly powerful book on the topic is *The Case for Faith* by Lee Strobel. Few people can have more powerful answers about God than a converted atheist.

It's one thing to accept that we don't have the power to always succeed. It's one thing to realize that we can't control the hearts of other human beings. We won't always move the status quo as far as we hope, and sometimes it will appear that nothing's changed at all (though that's rarely true). But it's quite another thing to be OK with this and choose to fight anyway.

I'll be honest. After losing the 2008 Colorado Personhood Campaign, I did comparatively little for a while. I struggled with my faith. It wasn't that I didn't believe in God anymore or that I doubted in Christ alone for my salvation; it wasn't that. Rather than the core doctrines of the Christian faith, it was my belief about how faith plays out in everyday life that was shaken to its core. I had to stop blaming God for people's actions and choices.

I came face to face with the reality of the hardness of the human heart. It's not a pretty sight, but it's an even greater reason to push forward. Yes, sin hardens the hearts of humankind. And yet somewhere deep within is also a heart that God created—a heart that *can* listen and accept the truth.

Giving up simply isn't an option. My only option is speaking, speaking again, and then speaking some more. My job is to speak until I have no voice, to write until I have no fingers, and to do justice until my life is spent.

I had thought faith was believing that God *will* do something. Instead, I realized faith is believing that God *can* do something without expecting Him to do it. I had to accept—in my heart and not just in my mind—that His ways are absolutely higher than mine. His understanding reaches far beyond me. His plans are better than mine, even when I don't see how. Right now I see dimly; one glorious day, I will see fully.

Believing that God can do the impossible is not wrong in the least. Yet faith is not simply believing that God will give us victory or render the results that we, in our short-sighted humanity, think are best. Can He? Yes. Is He powerful enough? Without a doubt. But our faith is misdirected when we transfer our own expectations to God. True faith is believing with all our hearts that God is with us in every moment and that He is able to make the impossible happen.

There is a huge difference between believing that God *can* and believing that God *will*. Consider the difference deeply. These concepts aren't things we can fully understand in our finite humanity, but they are things we can believe. As Pastor Richard Cimino puts it, "We do not live on explanations; we live on promises."[1]

Trying: Necessary to Faithfulness

Being faithful starts with discovering the passion in your heart. Every person has a God-given passion deep within his or her heart to serve and to change this world for Christ, and I believe we all can find it. God put the passion there, and He will finish the good work He has started. One thing matters: you are God's child, and with His power behind you, you are unstoppable through every obstacle and unbeatable through every loss.

Your part is to make an unwavering commitment to *trying*. And when you realize Who is behind you, with you, and before you, it's not a difficult commitment to make.

You know that saying "God is good, all the time. All the time, God is good"? It couldn't be truer, and it's something else we *must* believe. We must believe many things we might not understand. That's why it's called *faith*. As mere people, we have to put our "wisdom" concerning what's best aside and let God work. Often, we do not understand His purposes. They are beyond our comprehension. We cannot see as far as He sees—into the past or the future. *We are not God.* And therefore, we must do what we can, try what we may, and let God be God.

True faith—and the faithfulness born of trying and trusting—is richer and deeper and more infinitely beautiful than I knew at age twenty-one. And I'm sure I'll say the same thing if I ever make it to ninety-nine.

The two focuses we need to have in our fight for social justice are simple:

1. Life is about pleasing God.
2. Our job is simply to try our absolute best and to be faithful.

I believe that at the end of our lives, God will care far more whether we tried than whether we succeeded when the results were outside our reach. Throughout the Bible, it's clear that God doesn't ask His people to produce successful results in the world's eyes. Instead, He asks them to say yes to His call. So often, the story of biblical heroes isn't the story of their success—though they ultimately do experience it in some form—but the story of their faithful response to God's call:

- Abraham said yes long before he knew where God was taking him.
- David said yes as a young man, years before the dream of being king would ever be fulfilled.
- Noah said yes to being mocked by men—by the whole world—because that was the only way to be faithful to his unseen God.
- Joseph said yes to purity and obedience, even when it landed him in prison for years.

- Moses's many instances of saying yes to God are worth quoting directly, and this is only one example: "He chose to be mistreated along with the people of God rather than to enjoy the fleeting pleasures of sin. He regarded disgrace for the sake of Christ as of greater value than the treasures of Egypt, because he was looking ahead to his reward. By faith he left Egypt, not fearing the king's anger; he persevered because he saw him who is invisible" (Heb. 11:25–27).
- Esther said yes to pain and possible death so she could be the instrument of God to save her people.
- Prophet after prophet said yes even when their missions appeared confusing or uncertain. Hebrews 11 says that "through faith," they "administered justice" (Heb. 11:32–33).
- Priscilla and Aquila said yes to faithfully serving in their corner, even though they aren't the like famous, recognized Christians of the New Testament.
- Jesus Himself said yes to a humiliating and horrific death—a seeming failure in the world's eyes—so that, after His faithfulness, He could accomplish the greatest triumph in all of eternity.

Of course, before we ourselves can answer yes, we must hear the call. Remember that God shows all of us what to do in different ways. He is the living God, and His Spirit moves in His people. There's no one prescribed way He will speak to each one of us—just as there was no one prescribed way He spoke in the Bible. That's part of the beauty of the Christian life. It's a difficult and simple journey all at once. The listening and seeking draws us close to His side, showing us His heart for us personally and for all humanity.

Not every one of us will believe that we have heard directly from God in this fight for justice, but we don't have to hear directly from Him in order to act.

God already tells us enough about what His people need to do in His Word. Not having any clear personal direction is actually OK. I realize that's a somewhat novel thought to some Christians, but it's also very freeing. Yes, we ought to always pray and continually seek the Lord, but we also ought to *just start doing something*. The call might be much clearer than we've realized.

Before we were married, my husband taught me about this. He's a mover and a shaker for justice in his own right, and I love how he explains this concept of acting while seeking and of realizing the call God has already given us:

> The Lord already tells us what to do. Are we even faithful with that? Why would He tell us more? Love justice, seek mercy, defend those who can't defend themselves. He clearly tells us all of that, but are we already doing that? It's pretty clear. If we're not willing to step out in faith and do what the Bible's already so clear on us doing, why would He tell us more? Could it be true that He has already given us all the direction we need and is waiting for us to follow it? God doesn't owe specific direction to anyone. It's incredible when He gives it, but He doesn't owe it. If He never specifically directs me, I would still owe Him just as much, and I'd still be just as responsible for just as much. The Bible is clear: you're not living this life for your own selfish pleasures. Be faithful. Start moving. Do what you know is right. And God may give you specific direction as you go.

Indeed, there are countless Scriptures that instruct us on what Christians ought to be doing to do justice in this world. As we start acting on the Word the Lord has already given, we will realize that changing things might be more possible than we ever dreamed. Micah 6:8, Proverbs 31:8–9, 1 Timothy 5:8, Matthew 22:37–40, Isaiah 1:17, and Isaiah 56:1 are just a few examples outlining what Christians ought to do in this world. Which others can you find?

Tim Hansel said it well:

> Our hearts beat excitedly over stories of people like Abraham and Moses, yet we fail to recognize that they were as frail and nervous as we are. We stand in awe of Moses at the burning bush: Now there is a bush that burns, we say. I would like to be a bush like that, but I'm just a heap of ashes. And that's as far as we get. We discuss the phenomenon of what God can do in a life, tell amazing stories about it, praise it—but then resign ourselves to being nothing more than what we think we are, a mere bystander, resigned to sitting in the balcony among the spectators. But it is not the bush that sustains the flame. It is God in the bush, and so, any old bush will do![2]

We would do well to be the righteous man, spoken of in Proverbs, who falls seven times and yet rises again. We would do well to get up again tomorrow and take courage, as the Lord instructed Joshua: "Have I not commanded you? Be strong and courageous. Do not be afraid; do not be discouraged, for the LORD your God will be with you wherever you go" (Josh. 1:9).

And this same God—the One Who is with us at every moment and until the end—is the same God from Whom we can hope to hear these words at the end of our lives: "His master said to him, 'Well done, good and faithful servant. You have been faithful over a little; I will set you over much. Enter into the joy of your master'" (Matt. 25:23 ESV).

CHAPTER ELEVEN

How to Develop a Plan of Action

I am only one, but I am one. I can't do everything, but I can do something. The something I ought to do, I can do. And by the grace of God, I will.
—E. Hale

When we consider the stories of the experts and everyday people in this book—and in our own lives—we can conclude that there is no one "absolute plan" of action for all Christians to get involved in social justice. There's no exact formula that will take us from where we are today to fighting for Christian social justice tomorrow. God has created each of us uniquely, He works with and in each of us uniquely, and He has given each of us a unique life and a unique journey.

That's not to say that there isn't right and wrong, good ideas and bad, or proper steps and wastes of time. God certainly does lay out principles for us in His Word that can help us develop a plan of action as we seek His face and His Word for what He would have us do. We were *created* to do good works. When God thought of us, He planned out the good works we would do in His name. Doing justice is one of these good works—one of the ways we actively love others in Christ and serve Christ Himself.

There are several biblical attitudes that are important to develop while we work for social justice. We do not have to display each of these attitudes perfectly before we can start fighting for justice, but it's important for us to ask God to build these attitudes in our hearts. We need to check our hearts for proper motives as we go, seeking to become more like Christ each day.

A lack of a proper attitude or a partially selfish motivation shouldn't necessarily stop us from acting in service to others. In fact, feeling like we can't act because our motivation isn't 100 percent Christlike might be one way that Satan will try to stop us from doing justice. But the realization that our attitudes or motivations don't match up with God's should give us pause to examine our hearts, seek the face of God, and ask Him to do some heart surgery as we follow Him onto the path of justice.

I will talk first about three attitudes that are important for social justice fighters and then I'll cover four pitfalls to avoid. Next, I'll review some self-examination questions and ideas that are designed to help you decide on a plan of action. Finally, I'll ask that you spend some time looking up the verses for the journey at the end of this chapter. Choose these and other Scriptures to commit to your memory or read them again and again so you remain inspired to *do justice* your whole life long.

Three Biblical Attitudes for Social Justice Fighters

All these attitudes can be cultivated on our Christian walk. We can ask God which one to focus on in our lives right now.

Holiness

This attitude boils down to a basic question: How can I save/rescue/serve people in a right way? Simply put, holiness is right living—first before God and then before man. Because Jesus lived a truly holy life, He "grew in favor with God and man" (Luke 2:52).

Sometimes we will have to choose who to follow, as Peter and John did when they boldly proclaimed, "We ought to obey God rather than men" (Acts 5:29 KJV). Holy living means that our choices should be above reproach; whenever we commit a sin, we need to make it right. Naturally, in the fight for social justice, there will be *many* people who don't approve of our actions. But as long as we're treating them kindly, acting righteously, and keeping our conscience clear before God, we are acting in holiness and pleasing the One Who matters most.

We must seek the Lord and His Word to find the answers to the questions holiness confronts us with. We must be confident that we are acting righteously in God's sight and pleasing Him in our actions. On occasion, we will have to choose to either believe the words of the Christians who oppose us or be secure in our own belief that we are being obedient to God. When we are criticized or questioned by other Christians, we should be thankful for the reminder to examine our hearts and motives. They might be on to something that we need to change. But they also might be focusing much too closely on one aspect or application of holiness that they believe is supreme, despite what the Word of God actually teaches.

Christians in social justice work can easily become like the Pharisees—so steeped in the letter of the law that they forget the spirit in which it was created. Christians can also become compromised and sinful like the culture around us, forgetting that we will one day answer to God for the choices we make. Our personal lives must be a genuine reflection of God's holiness. What message do we communicate by fighting human trafficking while secretly indulging in pornography that strips the value and worth of people created by God and sometimes outright abuses and violates them? Do we toy with hypocrisy when we serve the poor and homeless during the week, but on the weekends, we get drunk and open ourselves to actions that would otherwise be unthinkable and that mar the name of Christ?

All too often, for the sake of getting more money or reaching more people, Christians agree to water down their evangelizing or skip it all together. They start believing that physical needs are more important than spiritual needs. That thinking creeps in to the whole work, and soon, they are helping people without Christ—even though they originally set out to serve God.

Holiness reminds us that God expands our borders, not our own actions through artificial, compromised means. In the end, we are accountable to God. We know that eternity is real. The people we are serving, saving, and rescuing have souls, and they will spend eternity in either heaven or hell. If we don't help bring them to Christ, what eternal good have we done?

This isn't to say we must lose all strategy, tact, and wisdom in how we operate and evangelize. We must consider these things and never forget the main mission of bringing Christ. Holiness before God is essential. Before Him alone, we stand or fall. In our work, we must continually seek the face of God and ask that Christ's righteousness shine forth.

Love

Without love, we have nothing (1 Cor. 13). This isn't the warm, fuzzy feeling of adoring another person; it's the sacrificial, agape love that God gives us and asks us to shower others with. It is based on self-sacrifice, and it is the essence of God because He is love (1 John 4:8). This is the love with which we are called to love our enemies and pray for their salvation. When was the last time you sent a tract or a kind note in the mail to an enemy of yours? When was the last time you refused to speak badly of him or her?

We must stop attacking people because we have been personally offended. A coalition isn't always necessary or possible in social justice work, but just because we can't work side by side with someone doesn't mean we can't love that person with the love of God. Refusing to let God love another human being through us—whether this person is a fellow social justice solider with whom we *hugely* disagree or Hitler himself—will only make us hardened and cold. God spreads His love out on all humanity; He loves each person He created. While we'll never be perfect, we should strive to be more like our Creator, asking Him to pour His sacrificial, everlasting love into our hearts, where it can flow out to our fellow man.

Love is the basic root from which doing justice must grow. It is out of a godly love for our fellow man that true compassion blooms. A sympathetic concern for suffering people is most useful when it stems from a love that is willing to sacrifice the self while seeing the potential God created in these people.

Humility

Pride can creep in quietly, unnoticed, until suddenly, it's the biggest elephant in the room, demanding recognition in a variety of ways. Conversely, humility is unassuming. It reminds us that God delivered us too; that we are unworthy servants (Luke 17:10), blessed to be able to follow God's call; that we are in need of a Savior; that we are not all-knowing, all-capable, and all-wise.

There was a time in my life when I prayed almost daily that God would crush my pride. Pride is ugly and harmful—to others and to ourselves. Humility, on the other hand, is like a beautiful violet that, even after you've stepped on its bloom, releases a sweet fragrance. Humility doesn't focus on "my" rights, "my" way, "my" ideas, "my" opinion, or "my" anything. This doesn't mean that there isn't a time to stand up for what we believe is best or the idea we think will succeed. Confidence isn't inherently bad, and it can be very different and separate from pride. In fact, publicly lowering ourselves and saying how bad and unwise and unskilled we are can also be a form of pride, as it can draw all the attention to "me."

Humility isn't always an exact action. Rather, it is an attitude of the heart that pushes the self down and lifts others up and Christ higher still. Webster's 1828 dictionary (a lovely old-school relic) defines humility this way,[1] reminding us of two key Scripture passages:

> In ethics, freedom from pride and arrogance; humbleness of mind; a modest estimate of one's own worth. In theology, humility consists in lowliness of mind; a deep sense of one's own unworthiness in the sight of God, self-abasement, penitence for sin, and submission to the divine will.
>
> Before honor is humility. (Prov. 15)
>
> Serving the Lord with all humility of mind. (Acts 20)

Four Pitfalls Social Justice Fighters Must Avoid

If we fall in these areas, our work, our relationships, and the reputation of Christ can be damaged.

Callousness

When you hear about the same tragedy over and over and over again; when you see the photos of damaged, torn bodies and the tears streaming down wounded faces; when you experience some of humanity's greatest suffering; when you hear others refuse to help because their football game or television show or big house or cozy life is more important, it's easy to become calloused. In fact, it's a natural reaction.

But callousness prevents us from fully experiencing and demonstrating the love and compassion of Christ. We might still help the suffering and oppressed, but we're distant and aloof. Callousness might creep in slowly, and that's exactly why we have to watch for it.

Callousness can affect our personal relationships. We might downplay the importance of something our spouse cares about because it's not as "big" and "important" as the suffering and injustice we deal with every day. We might tell our children that their hurt really isn't a big deal because, after all, we've seen far worse. Callousness puts a layer—first of plastic wrap, then of leather, then of steel—around our hearts. It blocks us from fully experiencing the giving and receiving in life's relationships. And it prevents the fullness of the love of Christ from flowing through us.

Compromise

Compromise usually eases into our lives in a sly, subtle way. Little by little, we justify unbiblical shortcuts until it's just a way of life. We start by failing to actually find out what God says about something, and we don't take the time to hit our knees in earnest prayer. We're tired of waiting, tired of searching, and tired of asking, so we choose the easy road—the one well-traveled. We might even make this choice in anger because we feel that God hasn't answered our questions in the way we've sought.

Once a part of our lives and work, compromise is a difficult thing to root out. We remember how "easy" it was, how much happier and agreeable everyone was, how much less our work seemed to cost. But compromise actually comes at a much higher price than we ever imagined. It is never worth it. One day, after a season or a life of concession, we will look back and see rubble and ruins where we thought we had built a castle of difference and a city of change.

Of course, unbiblical compromise is different from when we listen to our comrades' ideas and forge the way together through wise strategy. The dangerous compromise is when we agree to go against the Word of God and His principles to get a job done.

Divisiveness

A major pitfall in social justice work is the divisive spirit that permeates various movements. You have one trenched in organization over here, one stubborn lone ranger over there, and one all-knowing new player right here. Instead of rejoicing that we are made differently, that God has given us different callings, and that it's likely we will accomplish justice through a variety of means, we stomp our feet and declare that we have the one and only way to victory.

Exactly how much justice do we accomplish when we argue among ourselves? When we spend our fleeting time debating and accusing and campaigning against each other, where do our resources go? To the people in need? Or to promoting our own agenda and slamming someone else's? When we are divisive and participate in strife and infighting, we allow the enemy to put a stranglehold on the good we could be doing. Justice is stopped in its tracks while we fight tooth and nail to be right. It's just not worth the cost.

A discussion on the best use of resources and the best way to fight injustice is often necessary. But in the end, if we can't and don't agree, we need to stop wasting time and stop attacking each other. Go your way, and I'll go mine. God will direct each of us to accomplish His justice.

Arrogance

This is the basic pitfall of humanity. Most of our other problems stem from arrogance and the pride it generates.

I know better than he does.

I have a better solution—a better strategy—and I'm going to make sure she knows it.
I have this all figured out.
I'm essential to this work.
If it weren't for me, all this good wouldn't have been done.
They should be asking me for help.

Me, me, me.

If we're willing to really look for arrogance, it probably won't be hard to see this monster when it rears its head in our hearts. What might be hard is admitting it, asking for help to uproot it, and willingly choosing to toss it out. But if we truly want to do justice, this choice is one of the best ones we'll ever make.

If we don't control our arrogance, secret pride will lead us down a desperately dangerous road. Soon we will start to believe that we know better than God; we will declare that God Himself needs "me" to make things happen.

Developing Your Plan

Now, let's get to work. How are you going to *do* justice personally?

Ask Questions

Ask yourself how Jesus would act in this world. We all have our unique callings, but there are also issues of justice that all Christians should care about. David Schmidt, former managing editor of Live Action News, shares his thoughts: "Christians are called to care for the weak and defenseless, and the preborn child struggling for life certainly fits this description. Jesus in his ministry often cared for the basic, physical needs of those suffering. The most basic physical need, even before food and water, is the safety to live the next moment. That is why Christians should care deeply about ending the violence of abortion in addition to other work like feeding the hungry."[2]

How can we advance the most basic issues of justice—like the safety to live in the next moment? What group of people has God given you a passion for or lay on your heart? The group you feel called to serve might stay the same throughout your entire life. It might also change as God takes you somewhere new.

A list of possible groups would be longer than this book. If you don't have a people group that automatically comes to mind, start thinking and praying. Have a brainstorming session alone or with your close friends, family members, or mentors. Write a list of people groups that need justice. Spend some time finding out what the Bible says about these people groups or the justice related to them. Continue to pray about what people group and what justice actions God is calling you to.

As the body of Christ, we are called to serve every group of people in this world and show Christ to them. No group is unimportant or "less" than another. Everyone needs Christ. Every person is valuable, and every life counts. Of course, there are certainly some groups that need justice more desperately than others, so give that some thought and prayer. Remember that what the world calls *justice* is not always biblical justice. Our justice must match up with what God says is justice, so don't be afraid to pursue answers to the questions that will lead you to real justice.

Brainstorm Ideas

To turn your decision into action, match your selected people group with a need, interest, or activity. Maybe you can see a place for a hobby, talent, or skill you have. But look at *their* needs—the measurable, tangible ones, as well as the subtle and spiritual ones—ahead of your own preferences. See where the two can match.

You should also ask yourself the following questions: Where can you serve at this point and place in your life? What do you realistically have time for, and is it possible to make more time without neglecting your other responsibilities and commitments (like your family)? Keep in mind that it's not always about the amount of time or money we can give; it's about our heart. Pray through your options and then *get started.* To do justice, we must act.

David Schmidt explains the approach of working, trying, and *doing* until you find your niche:

> First understand that the pro-life movement [like many social justice movements] is a big movement that needs many sorts of people. Pro-life organizations range from pregnancy care centers that practically meet the needs of pregnant women to pro-life youth advocacy to political organizations. Volunteer with as many as you can and find where you fit.
>
> The key is taking the first step. Nothing will ever happen if you don't take the first step. Overcome your fear of the unknown and try something new, and you may find that the impact you can have is greater than you ever imagined. Changing the world is possible, but it won't happen if your intentions never turn into actions.[3]

What ideas do you have? Go ahead . . . brainstorm! Write the needs and ideas down, have discussions with your friends, write out goals for your justice life, ask your parents or other mentors for advice, start with something small if you need to, or take a risk and go big. Whatever you do, get busy and serve! There are people in this world who need Christ in *you.*

Suggested Action Points for the Justice Issues in This Book

Abortion

- *Distribute pro-life flyers.* These can be ones you design or ones that advertise for a crisis pregnancy center or abortion healing ministry in your area (check out http://www.optionline.org, http://www.standupgirl.com, and http://www.healingafter.com). Make a simple flyer showing the beauty of preborn life and the facts of fetal development, referring people to a website for more information.
- *Sponsor a pro-life billboard or other ad.* Financially support the beautiful and life-saving ads by Virtue Media (http://www.virtuemedia.org). Create your own audio, graphic, or video ads and see if radio stations, churches, and so on will air them. Spread them on social media.
- *Start an Embrace Grace or Teen Mother Choices chapter.* This is a practical and fun way to encourage women in your church to support pregnant moms who need help (see http://www.embracegrace.com and http://www.tmcint.org).
- *Start or join a Students for Life group on your campus.* You can also look into Medical Students for Life and Law Students for Life (http://www.studentsforlife.org). Another campus project is the Pregnant on Campus Initiative (http://www.pregnantoncampus.org). Get involved with Justice for All and their college campus tours (http://www.jfaweb.org).
- *Become a pro-life counselor—either in person, on the phone, or through chat.* Volunteer opportunities (and training) can be found at a crisis pregnancy center or through an organization like OptionLine or Pregnancy

Line. Remember that you want to give women and families the real facts about abortion and fetal development: they deserve to know, and this is not manipulative or self-serving. We can always give the truth in a compassionate way (see http://www.optionline.org or http://www.pregnancyline.com).

- *Spread the word about abortion reversal.* The effects of an abortion pill can be reversed. Volunteers are needed for the twenty-four-hour hotline at http://www.abortionpillreversal.com, 1-877-558-0333. Search for abortion reversal stories online and spread them through social media.
- *Fundraise for or adopt an ultrasound bus.* These are run by Save the Storks or ICU Mobile (see http://www.savethestorks.com or http://www.icumobile.org).
- *Research.* Study the facts about abortion risks, fetal development, and hormonal birth control, IUDs, and the Morning After Pill and how these can be dangerous to women and take the life of a growing human being in the womb.
- *Show pro-life films.* The short films "Crescendo" (http://www.cpcmovie.com and free on YouTube) and "Mitosis" (http://www.mitosismovie.com and free on YouTube) are good examples to show to a group or at a fundraiser. Both were designed to be used to raise money for pregnancy resource centers.
- *Encourage your pastor, youth leader, or Bible study leader to give a pro-life sermon, talk, or Bible study.* If he or she will not, ask if you can present. Find out if you can set up a table, make a bulletin insert, or hand out brochures with pro-life educational information.

Foster Care and Adoption

- *Research.* Check out Project 1.27's comprehensive list of ideas to serve foster and adopted children and their families here: http://project127.com/wp-content/uploads/November-is-Adoption-Month.pdf.
- *Become a mentor or tutor for at-risk children.* Heather N. Taussig, PhD, from the Kempe Center for the Prevention and Treatment of Child Abuse and Neglect at the University of Colorado School of Medicine, conducted a study on the effects of mentoring and skills development on children in foster care. After seeing positive results, she believes that "even for the most vulnerable children, rigorous intervention efforts can make a difference and may lead to better outcomes and healthier futures."[4]
- *Choose child advocacy as your career.* According to the National Court Appointed Special Advocate Association (CASA for Children), "1,900 children become victims of abuse or neglect" every day in the United States, but CASA advocates are their voice.[5]

Human Trafficking

* Special thanks to Tom Tillapaugh for many of these ideas.

- *Encourage or put appropriate pressure on your local government officials.* Ask them to dedicate a task force—sometimes called "human trafficking units"[6] to stopping human trafficking and rescuing victims.
- *Start at home.* Educate your own daughters and, with their parents' permission, her friends about the tactics of pimps and others who traffic girls. Get educated about the extensiveness of trafficking by finding the most recent Trafficking in Persons Report online, put out by the U.S. Department of State.

- *Become a mentor, friend, teacher, or substitute parent for at-risk youth.* Provide educational, vocational, creative, and constructively fun opportunities, along with guidance, so they don't become the trafficked or the traffickers.
- *Reach out to hotels, truck stops, and trucking companies.* Design a program (or become familiar with one that already exists) that teaches hotel workers or truck drivers how to spot a trafficked girl or her pimp and how to notify law enforcement. Convince the hotels, truck stops, and trucking companies in your area to train their employees and implement a basic identification or rescue programs. Ask hotels, motels, and truck stops to put up an easy-to-see sign in their lobby or out by the road that lists the Human Trafficking Hotline (1-888-3737-888) and the BeFree Textline (233733).
- *Invent a system to find trafficking victims and their traffickers online.* Use the traffickers' online advertising against them and make it an effective way to find and rescue the victims. Work in cooperation with law enforcement. Check out the work of Ashton Kutcher's Thorn (http://www.wearethorn.org) and Operation Underground Railroad (http://www.ourrescue.org).
- *Spread the truth that pornography, strip clubs, and other such places support human trafficking and sex slavery.* Be an outspoken voice against these things—publicly, in church, online, or with your friends and family. Fight the New Drug (http://www.fightthenewdrug.org) is a great resource.
- *Evaluate your own life.* Are you participating in anything—porn, strip clubs, casino gambling, or something less obvious—that aids human trafficking? No, gambling doesn't specifically traffic girls, but many trafficked girls

are brought in where there is gambling. Is any level of participation OK with you? As a Christian, should we participate in any activity that encourages the enslavement of people? Do we have a duty to speak the truth to our friends as well?

Women's Rights

- *Host a bake sale.* You can raise money for women's projects and educate people about true justice for women at the same time. Pass out flyers and ask people to read them.
- *Dedicate a weekly Facebook post, tweet, Instagram, or text to your friends to real issues of women's justice.* Include a source each time where they can get more information or where they can help—or get help if they are a victim.
- *Show informative films.* Host get-togethers with your friends, churchgoers, club members, or family where you show documentaries like *It's a Girl!* or *Veil of Tears* so people are educated on the real War on Women.
- *Donate to women's projects that promote life for all.* Some good works are sponsored and run by trusted organizations like Samaritan's Purse, Transworld Radio, or Compassion International.
- *Provide supplies for a pregnant mothers' home.* You can also look into providing for a rescue center for trafficking victims or a women's shelter where abused women flee with their children.
- *Reach out.* Teach life skills to needy women.
- *Raise the next generation of women with a biblical view of feminism and justice for women.* Help them see that Jesus was one of the biggest advocates for women's true and meaningful equality in all of history.

- *Work with an organization to bring women and girls out of Mormon or Muslim polygamy.* Help them develop the skills and the financial support they need to start a new life.
- *Never forget the power of the gospel and the love of Jesus.* Make this an essential part of your service to women.

Poverty, Homelessness, and Refugees

- *Work to promote marriage and families.* Strong family units and solid marriages are one key to battling poverty, particularly in the United States.
- *Persist in your own marriage or in purity as a single person.* Save sex for marriage. Model to the world what a true, faithful, Christian marriage looks like.
- *Support important programs.* Initiatives like Compassion's Child Survival Program aid pregnant mothers and young children so that they can survive and be provided with nutrition, education, and medical care.
- *Start or work at a community garden.* Provide the poor with healthful food and minister to their spiritual needs at the same time.
- *Volunteer with a ministry that aligns with proper principles of justice, including being pro-life.* Also choose a ministry that believes in the unifying and reconciling power of the gospel and isn't afraid to openly witness in truth and love to those they serve.
- *Start an internship program at your work.* Bring in a teenager from a poor family, a single mom, or an unemployed dad and teach them a new job while mentoring them.
- *Give money.* Bringing justice to refugees requires a lot of on-the-ground work, and organizations like Samaritan's Purse bring the people and supplies in. But naturally, they

need money to do their work. Samaritan's Purse is also particularly committed to bringing the gospel too.

- *Take on political work.* Find out how to get the United States to allow more refugees to resettle here.
- *Be the personal Christian connection and friend that refugees need.* There are definite communities of refugees, specifically in large cities. You can find them and go to them. Offer them friendship and the love of Christ. Do what you can to meet their material, spiritual, and emotional needs. Break down the barriers. Some will have suffered great persecution for Christ or for other reasons in their own nations, and there is much you can learn from them too.

People with Disabilities

* Special thanks to Leticia Velasquez, founder of KIDS (Keep Infants with Down Syndrome), and to Cassy Fiano for a number of the ideas and resources that follow.

- *Don't be afraid to share.* Publicly share your story of giving life to a child with a disability.
- *Broadcast on social media.* Create graphics and shareable photos for Instagram and Flickr, compose Tweets, write Facebook posts, and help spread the beauty of life for people with disabilities. Remember those at the end of life too.
- *Prayerfully consider adopting a child with disabilities—locally or internationally.* Many international children languish in orphanages because of a disability that could be easily cared for in the United States.
- *Find a way to fund medical help and care for children with disabilities whose families are struggling.* One way is to support Samaritan's Purse's Children's Heart Project (through a donation or through opening your home).

- *Speak out and campaign against euthanasia and physician-assisted suicide.* Tell the real stories on this issue, remembering how vulnerable people are pressured to end their lives and made to believe they are a burden.
- *Sign up for Google alerts whenever Down syndrome appears in the news.* When articles arrive in your inbox, go to them and comment to encourage expectant moms to give birth to babies with Down syndrome. You could do this for any disability.
- *Ask your church to host a "Beautiful Disabilities" Sunday, event, or banquet.* Get your friends on board—or pioneer it alone—and plan it.
- *Educate people on the help and health care options available for parents with children who have disabilities.* Focus on ensuring that pregnant mothers and parents whose preborn babies have just been diagnosed with a disability are being informed of their child's true possibilities and the value of his or her life. Often, these parents are pushed into a rush decision for abortion without all the information.
- *Start a website for parents whose preborn children have just been diagnosed with a disability.* Give them hope and point them to real medical and financial help. The medical field has been transformed in recent years, with many options for people with disabilities. A hopeful future is possible, and parents need to know this.
- *Guide others to information.* Be familiar with informative, pro-life resources you can direct a friend to if their preborn baby is ever diagnosed with a disability.
- *Start or work with the First Call Program in your state.* If an expectant parent's child is diagnosed with Down

syndrome, they will be matched with another parent whose child also has Down syndrome, so they can get firsthand information from someone who's already been in that situation. While some in this program might unfortunately suggest abortion as an option, the program's intention is for parents to get factual and modern information about Down syndrome so they can be empowered to raise their child alongside a supportive community.

Acting on the Plan

One of the main things required in action is courage. Sometimes courage isn't a big, loud, brave thing; it's a quiet, faithful thing that keeps plodding along, despite the obstacles in our path.

- *Just do it.* Send that e-mail. Make that phone call. Go have that meeting. Set up your event. Launch your website. Just do it. Do justice today. Pray, plan, and ask for wise advice, but don't overthink. Good preparation is essential, but too much thought can prevent action.
- *Write out your plan.* Write out your steps of action. Step by step, day by day, we are *doing*. We are *acting*. We are bringing change and justice. So even if it's a small step, write it down. Go do it, cross it off, and then do the next step. This way, you'll see right in front of your eyes what exactly is required to act on your plan. You'll see that you are doing it. And you'll be encouraged to keep it going.
- *Find justice friends.* Bring people along with you. Instead of meeting up with your friend for coffee every week, you could work on a justice project together instead. Do you have a friend who wants something more to do with their life? Do you know someone with a skill or talent that could be used for justice? You will both be encouraged

and motivated. Sometimes the journey will be lonely. But the Lord will remind us that we do not walk alone. Just as He reminded Elijah, there are thousands more who also serve the one true God, even when we can't see them.

- *Stay filled up.* As you act on your plan, remember to take some time to allow yourself to be filled up. Read the Word. Listen to biblical teaching. Worship. Turn on the Christian station as you drive. Meet with friends who make you laugh or who make you dinner. Have a social outlet or a fun hobby if you need one. When we are full, we can pour out. When we enjoy the beautiful life we've been given, we can bring beauty to others as well.
- *Keep Scripture in front of you.* The Word of God is powerful—more than we can fully realize. And His Word is what will truly inspire us to remain faithful, to stay in the battle, and to not give up. His Word tells us that we are not alone, we are held, we are loved, we are called. There is a reason for justice. And there will be a victory for justice. We will see it with our own eyes.

Verses for the Journey

Now, take some time to look up the following verses for your justice expedition. Write down your own and tape them up on your bathroom mirror or on the wall by your kitchen sink, put them in your wallet or your glove box, save them as your lock screen—whatever will help you see them when you need them the most.

- Deuteronomy 15:11
- 1 Samuel 2:24
- 2 Chronicles 15:7
- Proverbs 31:8–9
- Haggai 1:7

- Matthew 5:16
- Matthew 6:33
- Matthew 10:42
- Matthew 20:28
- Matthew 25:40
- Matthew 28:19
- Mark 10:45
- Luke 10:30–37
- Luke 21:1–4
- Acts 20:35
- Romans 12:1–21
- Romans 12:6
- Romans 12:9–13
- 1 Corinthians 9:19
- Galatians 6:2
- Ephesians 2:10
- Philippians 2:3
- 1 Timothy 6:17–19
- 2 Timothy 1:9
- Titus 3:14
- Hebrews 6:10–12
- Hebrews 10:24
- Hebrews 13:1–5
- Hebrews 13:16
- James 1:2–5
- James 2:14–17
- 1 John 3:17–18

CHAPTER TWELVE

Why We Fight

Sometimes standing against evil is more important than defeating it. The greatest heroes stand because it is right to do so, not because they believe they will walk away with their lives. Such selfless courage is a victory in itself.
—N. D. Wilson

I keep four things on my dresser (well, more than four, but there are only four I'm going to tell you about). They remind me what I'm fighting for as I seek to do justice, why I'm fighting, and Who has called me and is with me in this lifelong fight.

First up is a round, smooth stone with the reference "1 Samuel 17:40–49" printed on it. You'll recall that this is the story of the little shepherd boy, David, who fought the mighty giant, Goliath. This stone was given to me by a kind friend during the Personhood campaign. It reminds me that God doesn't always use the great, predictable things that we humans place our trust in to bring about His justice. Sometimes He uses the small, seemingly powerless things—and the little, weak people too.

We must courageously follow where He leads, no matter how terrifying the evil we face. Because, in the end, it is God Himself

Who brings the ultimate victory. This little stone reminds me of God, of fearlessness, of trust, of boldness to speak, and of faithfulness.

Next is another stone (you'd think I have a thing for rocks). This one is made of some sort of metal, and I bought it not long after seeing *The Passion of the Christ*. The words of Isaiah 53:5 are etched on the back: "He was pierced for our transgressions, He was crushed for our iniquities, the punishment that brought us peace was upon Him, and by His wounds we are healed." Is there a more beautiful verse in the Bible?

We are able to do justice in this world only because of Christ's sacrifice on our behalf. He led the way, taking the price that justice required upon Himself. By trusting in Christ alone for salvation, we are saved. This metal stone reminds me that Christ is my rock and my sole basis for salvation, for living each day, and for loving others and doing justice in a suffering world. He is my example, and I pray that I will follow in His footsteps until my journey on earth is over.

Third in my little collection is a small red button printed with the face of a preborn child and the words "Personhood Now!" This reminds me of two things: first, now is always the right time to do what's right; and second, no matter where I go, my heart will always be with the preborn. I am convinced that God has called me to fight for their deliverance, and I cannot stop until abortion ends. Millions of innocent human beings have lost their lives in cruel and unspeakable ways, and too few know the truth. This killing is one of the largest genocides in human history, and it continues today. Until our preborn children are recognized as equal human beings under the law, I cannot end my fight for their justice. And I pray you won't neglect them either.

Fourth and last is the newest piece on my dresser: a *Hunger Games* pin (cue the Katniss Everdeen groupie jokes). My husband, knowing me extremely well, gave me this on our fifth anniversary.

The pin reminds me of the message of revolution. A revolution is a "turnaround" and a "fundamental change." If ever a revolution were needed in the social justice world, it's today. Too many people groups are excluded from the reach of the typical calls for social justice. Too few evangelicals have believed that, as conservatives, they have a place at the table—a place they must insist on taking.

An old friend of mine once told me that as Christians, our job isn't merely to sit at the table. Our job is to be at the head of the table. And then we want to make sure the person sitting next to us is a Christian too. Finally, we want to make sure everyone sitting at the table is a Christian. That's the way we influence the world.

Now, my friend wasn't saying that Christians should steamroll over everyone or that anyone who's not a Christian is someone we should throw out. On the contrary, there are two lessons I've taken out of what he said. First, Christians shouldn't be content to follow when they're called to lead. Second, we should either bring other Christians with us or be such a loving and persuasive witness to those around us that they *become* Christians by our words and example. Remember: we are to be wise as serpents and gentle as doves.

And so it must be in this work of doing justice. We must take part in the revolution of true, conservative, compassionate justice, and we must bring others along with us. Be the spark. Jesus Himself affirmed that even with only a little faith, He can take care of the rest: "Truly I tell you, if you have faith as small as a mustard seed, you can say to this mountain, 'Move from here to there,' and it will move. Nothing will be impossible for you" (Matt. 17:20). So as long as we live, let us have at least a little faith, rely on our Savior, and bring life to the justice revolution.

Outside the Camp

Hebrews 13:12–13 describes how Jesus was willing to go outside the camp—to be disgraced and to do the abnormal thing—for the sake of those who were in great need: "And so Jesus also suffered outside the city gate to make the people holy through his own blood. Let us, then, go to him outside the camp, bearing the disgrace he bore." Christians also must be willing to be disgraced, dishonored, ridiculed, and misunderstood in our quest to serve God.

Are you called to stand outside an abortion clinic and deal directly with the women seeking an abortion *in that very moment*? Are you called to go to India and personally rescue young girls from sex slavery, like Amy Carmichael did? Are you called to be a foot soldier, an on-the-ground-rescuer? Are you called to risk your life and your own well-being like Dr. Kent Brantly, who treated victims of the Ebola epidemic in Liberia? Were you made to burn with those who burn or to pull them from the very flames that threaten to rage against them and overtake them? And don't just choose this type of social justice work because it sounds nobler upfront.

Every piece of the puzzle, every part of the body of Christ, every task involved in the work of doing justice is of equal importance. And each work is necessary. Those on the front lines couldn't go out and fight without the work of those who stay behind. So without letting pride overtake you or fear suffocate you, seek God in the work you are uniquely designed to carry out. Do your research, partner with the right people and organizations, or be willing to go alone if necessary. Be willing to burn with those who burn if it comes to that.

Those who serve God at home and those who serve Him far away are often equally disgraced. It doesn't matter where we go, but rather, Who we follow. We fight for justice to follow our Savior. Being willing to go "outside the camp" captures the idea of being willing to go where others will not, of being willing to follow the Lord to the places *He* deems worthy. Sometimes these places are ordinary and closer to home than we expect. Other times, they are farther away than we ever imagined.

Outside the Camp

"Unclean!" "Unclean!" the crowd's cruel cry
The leper shrinks into the shade
"Away!" "Be gone!" the rocks still fly
And cut the flesh from which life fades.

"No hope!" "Not her!" no one believes
This child will live to see the dawn
Away they turn to homes of ease
Leaving her a devil's pawn

"His blood!" "It flows!" into the street
No one knows it is him—a man
The wounds, the wounds, such pain so deep
Does salvation have a plan?

"I've come!" "I see!" a new Voice cries
Running outside the city gate
"God will heal and they will rise!"
Deliverance cannot wait.

Leper, the child, man with wounds
Before they breathe their very last
From death, from hell, at last unbound
Still scorning crowds stand aghast.

Maybe no one understands
Maybe no one's hearts are touched
But we can see an outstretched hand
And we cannot love too much

Jesus knows, He was the first
To go outside the camp of men
To men beyond who suffered worst
And there we too, are truly sent.[1]

Roses and Bearing Our Crosses with Honor

If you came to my house, you'd find roses in nearly every room. This elegant flower holds wonderful memories for me: That first rose on my seat on our first date. Those two roses on my seat the day he asked me to marry him. The bunches of tiny baby roses he gave me when I graduated from law school, more than seven months pregnant with our daughter. The roses he chose for me with our baby son for the first time.

And the rose that sits on our fireplace mantel, reminding me of a life saved.

One day, a young woman wrote to me on my personal blog. She asked me for advice because she was pregnant and wanted to keep her baby, but her boyfriend was pushing her to have an abortion. She didn't think she could tell her parents because they'd be furious with her. After exchanging prayers and e-mails, she realized she was strong and that she could give her baby life. *She* was her baby's mother, and no one could take that from her. I believe that every woman has a God-given strength to stand up for the life of her child and defend him or her. But sometimes, we women need to be reminded of this strength.

This young mother chose life for her baby, despite her boyfriend's and parents' disapproval and anger. A major turning point for her was hearing the heartbeat of her baby girl. Her boyfriend ended up coming around, but I'm not sure if her parents ever did. While she was still pregnant, she wrote to another young mother, expressing her confidence that her little girl would have her love, no matter what else she might lack. She encouraged the other mother to hear her baby's heartbeat, explaining that it was the "most amazing thing I have ever experienced and the reason I am now going to raise my daughter on my own."

When her daughter was born, she gave her the middle name Rose.

It's amazing and miraculous when God uses us to save another human being's life. It's also heartbreaking when a life isn't saved.

Another young girl wrote me, and we racked up more than sixty e-mails in the span of little more than two weeks. At the time, I was actually pregnant with my own son, though I didn't know it yet. As this new life grew inside of me, I fought for another life. I know there is nothing more I could have done to save Robbie—the name she gave her son before she aborted him—but *oh, how I wish there was.*

For my birthday the next year, my husband gave me an Amazon gift card (you're probably getting the picture that he knows me *quite* well), and I bought a beautiful Precious Moments angel who is holding a baby with the words "Sleep in Heavenly Peace" on it. I keep this little memorial of Robbie on my fireplace mantel, right next to my rose.

This is how the fight for social justice goes. From joyful salvation, to heartrending defeat and failure, and back again to joyful salvation. When we become deeply invested in the fight, we feel the failures more deeply. While self-examination and evaluation of situations is important, we can waste so much time dwelling on the "if-I had-only-done-this-differently" thought process. We must allow ourselves to grieve—maybe once, maybe regularly. But we also must move ahead.

There are *always* more lives to be saved; *always* more victories to be had; and yes, probably always more failures as well. But when we choose to fight for social justice in this sin-hardened world, we choose to suffer the pain of failure. We choose to bear this cross. It is a worn, splintered, and outright dirty cross, but it is also holy and beautiful. We can bear it with honor because the empty grave promises that life eternal is coming.

Conclusion

So why do we do justice? We do justice because we have been called. We do justice because we must be faithful. We do justice because this sinful world is full of injustice and oppression. We do justice because there are needs and issues and injustices bigger than ourselves. And we do justice because, like Jesus, *we love.* In fact, the "why" of fighting for social justice can be summed up in two words that Jesus often spoke and that He still speaks today: "Follow Me."

Our first choice to follow Jesus involved our salvation. When we said, "Yes, I need Jesus. I can't save myself. I'm not good enough alone. I sin. I'm in need of a Savior," we were saved. Our salvation is found in Christ alone, through His grace alone—our salvation is not dependent on our good works. And yet, we should choose to follow Christ further; to follow Him into the good works He chose for us when He created us (Eph. 2:10).

The choice to follow Jesus is also a continual, daily choice. The choice to serve others, to meet needs, and to do good works—to do justice—isn't what saves us, but it is what shows the world around us that we are truly followers of Christ.

Today, will we hoist our cross onto our backs, bearing the weight, the shame, and the honor? Today, will we follow in the footsteps of Christ, even if we don't know where He is leading? Today, are we willing to follow Him to dark and untouched cities; will we serve at home or in the corner He has placed us? Today, will we follow Him, even though we struggle with selfish desire, prideful motivation, or crippling fear? Today, will we follow Him when it means saying no to self and yes to those who are truly in need?

Today, what is our choice?

When we follow, we don't always see the victory. We don't usually know what's going to be required of us. We can't often predict the sacrifices that will be needed or the greatness of the reward. In fact, there's very little that we know. But we can always be confident of two things: Christ, Who has called, is faithful; and Christ, Who is leading, has already won. Death and the grave have no power over Him; neither do fear, oppression, and injustice. And so they have no power over us.

Our task is simple, but taking it up is one of the hardest choices we will ever make. Will you follow Him, wherever He leads, whatever it costs? Will you choose not just to start well but—by the grace of God—to finish well too? Ask yourself if you are ready to do what Jesus required of his disciples in Matthew 16:24 (NLT): "Then Jesus said to his disciples, 'If any of you wants to be my follower, you must turn from your selfish ways, take up your cross, and follow me.'"

Notes

Chapter One

[1]Megan Carpentier, "They Just Won't Quit," *Wonkette*, December 11, 2007, http://wonkette.com/332566/they-just-wont-quit.

[2]Boylanz, "Cracker of the Week: Kristi Burton," *Opting: In or Out*, December 12, 2007, http://optinginorout.blogspot.com/2007/12/cracker-of-week-kristi-burton.html.

[3]Electa Draper, "Face of 'Personhood' Issue Young, Resolute," *Denver Post*, May 4, 2008, http://www.denverpost.com/2008/05/04/face-of-personhood-issue-young-resolute/.

[4]Megan Carpentier, "Kristi Burton Is Not Exactly Beloved by the Anti-Abortion Movement," *Jezebel*, November 3, 2008, http://jezebel.com/5075010/kristi-burton-is-not-exactly-beloved-by-the-anti-abortion-movement.

[5]Adam Cayton-Holland, "Meet Kristi Burton, the 21-Year-Old Pro-Lifer behind the Personhood Amendment," *Denver Westword News*, September 25, 2008, http://www.westword.com/news/meet-kristi-burton-the-21-year-old-pro-lifer-behind-the-personhood-amendment-5100826.

[6]Sarah Kliff, "Roe v. Wade v. Kristi," *Newsweek*, October 31, 2008.

[7]Fred Barnes, "Maverick for Life," *Weekly Standard*, September 1, 2008, http://www.weeklystandard.com/maverick-for-life/article/16597.

[8]Sarah Ray (executive director, Yobel International), in discussion with the author, February 2015.

Chapter Two

[1]Gene Roncone (lead pastor, Highpoint Church), in discussion with author, December 2014.

[2]Seth Silvers (founding partner and CEO, Story On), in discussion with author, December 2014.

[3]Reggie Littlejohn (founder and president, Women's Rights Without Frontiers), in discussion with author, February 2015.

[4]Robert Gelinas (lead pastor, Colorado Community Church; founder, Project 1.27), in discussion with author, January 2015.

[5]Quin Friberg (apologist, FWC Apologetic Ministries), in discussion with author, March 2015.

[6]Bethany Hoang, *Deepening the Soul for Justice* (Downers Grove, IL: InterVarsity Press, 2012).

[7]"Personal History of Prophet Jeremiah," *Holy Spirit Advantage Prophetic Ministries*, accessed October 26, 2014, http://www.hsapm.org/jeremiahslife.html.

[8]Gladys Aylward with Christiane Hunter, *Gladys Aylward: The Little Woman* (Chicago: Moody Press, 1970).

[9]Eustace Carey, *Memoir of William Carey, D. D.: Late Missionary to Bengal, Professor of Oriental Languages in the College of Fort William, Calcutta* (Boston: Gould, Kendall, and Lincoln, 1836).

[10]Sam Wellman, *Mary Slessor: Queen of Calabar* (Uhrichsville, OH: Barbour Paperback, 1998).

[11]Jodi Visser (family friend), in discussion with author, 2014.

[12]Ibid.

[13]Greg Stier (CEO and founder, Dare 2 Share Ministries), in discussion with author, February 2015.

[14]Ibid.

Chapter Three

[1]"Rwandan Genocide," *Wikipedia*, last modified January 26, 2017, http://en.wikipedia.org/wiki/Rwandan_Genocide.

[2]National Right to Life Committee, "U.S. Abortion Statistics by Year (1973–Current)," *Christian Life Resources*, January 2016, http://www.christianliferesources.com/article/u-s-abortion-statistics-by-year-1973-current-1042.

[3]"Number of Abortions, Abortion Counters," *US Abortion Clock*, http://www.numberofabortions.com.

[4]The real details of abortion and the stories behind the procedure can be easily found online, particularly from the doctors and nurses who performed abortions for years and bravely left the clinics. Their reasons for quitting are varied, but it almost always related to a personal experience of the humanity of these tiny persons. See the testimony of Dr. Anthony Levatino, former Planned Parenthood director Abby Johnson, Dr. David Brewer, former clinic owner Carol Everett, nurse Marianne Anderson, Dr. Bernard Nathanson, Dr. Vansen Wong, and the nurses of Douglas Karpen's clinic.

[5]Christina Marie Bennett (journalist at Live Action News, Bound4Life, http://www.chrismarie.com, and more; client service manager at ABC Women's Center), in discussion with author, March 2015.

[6]Most people understand *conception* to mean "fertilization"—the earliest beginning of a new human life and the start of pregnancy. However, some hormonal birth control manufacturers use a redefinition of conception and pregnancy, claiming that it begins at implantation. Implantation occurs several

days after the new human life has begun. Using this redefinition enables the birth control manufacturers to claim that their pill or device does not end a pregnancy, whereas some scientific studies show that it actually can. Women deserve the full facts on birth control, and this and additional information is available in Abby Johnson, "A Comprehensive Look at Contraception," March 17, 2015, http://www.abbyjohnson.org/discussions-2/2015/3/31/discussions-test-post; and Randy Alcorn, "Does the Birth Control Pill Cause Abortions?," *Eternal Perspective Ministries*, 2011, http://store.epm.org/product/does-the-birth-control-pill-cause-abortions.

[7] Jan Langman, *Medical Embryology*, 3rd ed. (Baltimore: Williams and Wilkins, 1975), 3.

[8] Ronan O'Rahilly and Fabiola Muller, *Developmental Stages in Human Embryos* (Washington, DC: Carnegie Institution of Washington, 1987).

[9] Keith L. Moore and T. V. N. Persaud, *Before We Are Born: Essentials of Embryology and Birth Defects*, 4th ed. (Philadelphia: W. B. Saunders, 1993), 1.

[10] Jérôme Lejeune, "21 Thoughts," Association Les Amis Du Professeur Jérôme Lejeune, http://amislejeune.org/index.php/en/jerome-lejeune/jerome-lejeunes-message/textes-and-quotations/thoughts/.

[11] "Report of the South Dakota Task Force to Study Abortion," December 2005, http://www.dakotavoice.com/Docs/South%20Dakota%20Abortion%20Task%20Force%20Report.pdf.

[12] Planned Parenthood v. Rounds, No. 05-3093 (8th Cir. June 27, 2008), http://media.ca8.uscourts.gov/opndir/08/06/053093P.pdf.

[13] "First of Our Three Billion Heartbeats Is Sooner than We Thought," *University of Oxford*, October 11, 2016, http://www.ox.ac.uk/news/2016-10-11-first-our-three-billion-heartbeats-sooner-we-thought.

[14] Kristi Burton Brown, "5 Little-Known Facts about Planned Parenthood," *Live Action News*, February 5, 2015, http://liveactionnews.org/five-little-known-facts-about-planned-parenthood.

[15] For the most up-to-date information on the congressional hearings related to Planned Parenthood, visit "House Investigation into Planned Parenthood," *House Republicans*, accessed December 23, 2016, https://www.gop.gov/solution_content/plannedparenthood.

[16] Richard Dahlstrom, *O2: Breathing New Life into Faith* (Eugene, OR: Harvest House, 2008).

[17] Lila Rose (founder and president, Live Action News), in discussion with author, February 2015.

[18] Ibid.

[19] Ibid.

[20] Ibid.

[21] Jill L. Stanek, "Testimony of Jill L. Stanek, RN IL Senate Health & Human Services Committee," *Illinois Senate*, March 12, 2003, http://www.jillstanek.

com/Testimony%2C%20IL%20Senate%20Health%20%26%20Human%20 Services%2C%203-12-03.pdf.

[22] John McCormack, "Video: Planned Parenthood Official Argues for Post-Birth Abortion," *Weekly Standard*, March 29, 2013, http://www.weeklystandard.com/blogs/video-planned-parenthood-official-argues-right-post-birth-abortion_712198.html.

[23] Jill Stanek (national campaign chair, Susan B. Anthony List), in discussion with author, January 2015.

[24] Ibid.

[25] Ibid.

[26] "SBA List Young Leaders Award Winners Announced," *SBA List*, March 12, 2014, http://www.sba-list.org/newsroom/news/sba-list-young-leader-award-winners-announced.

[27] Steven Ertelt, "NARAL Prez to Resign: Says Pro-Choice Side Getting Too Old," *LifeNews*, May 10, 2012, http://www.lifenews.com/2012/05/10/naral-pro-abortion-prez-to-resign-for-younger-replacement.

[28] Bethany Goodman (assistant director, March for Life), in discussion with author, January 2015.

[29] Claire Chretien (correspondent, LifeSiteNews), in discussion with author, January 2015.

[30] Goodman, discussion with author.

[31] Chretien, discussion with author.

[32] Goodman, discussion with author.

[33] Chretien, discussion with author.

[34] Goodman, discussion with author.

[35] Seth Drayer (director of training, Created Equal), in discussion with author, March, 2015.

[36] Ibid.

Chapter Four

[1] Congressional Coalition on Adoption Institute, http://www.ccainstitute.org.

[2] National Center for Child Welfare Excellence, "An Overview of Placement Stability," http://www.nccwe.org/toolkits/placement-stability/overview.htm.

[3] Congressional Coalition on Adoption Institute, "Fact Sheets: U.S. Adoption and Foster Care Statistics," http://www.ccainstitute.org/resources/fact-sheets.

[4] Ibid.

[5] Tennyson Center for Children at Colorado Christian Home, "Child Abuse in America," https://www.childabuse.org/facts.

[6]Centers for Disease Control and Prevention, "Child Abuse and Neglect: Consequences," last updated April 5, 2016, https://www.cdc.gov/violenceprevention/childmaltreatment/consequences.html.

[7]Congressional Coalition on Adoption Institute, http://www.ccainstitute.org/index.php?option=com_content&view=category&layout=blog&id=25&Itemid=43.

[8]Cynthia McFadden, "Foster-Care System Stretched Too Far," *ABC News*, July 2, 2016, http://abcnews.go.com/WNT/story?id=130266.

[9]See, for example, the CASA for Children homepage at http://www.coloradocasa.org.

[10] American Academy of Child and Adolescent Psychiatry, "Facts for Families: Foster Care," May 2005, updated February 2013, http://www.aacap.org/AACAP/Families_and_Youth/Facts_for_Families/Facts_for_Families_Pages/Foster_Care_64.aspx#contentstart.

[11]Veronica M. Cruz, "Parental Substance Abuse the Main Reason Kids End Up in Foster Care," *Arizona Daily Star*, December 9, 2013, http://tucson.com/news/local/parental-substance-abuse-the-main-reason-kids-end-up-in/article_9add334f-8496-5ada-a4bf-35aabeda024f.html.

[12] "Facts on Foster Care in America," *ABC News*, May 30, 2006, http://abcnews.go.com/Primetime/FosterCare/story?id=2017991&page=1.

[13]Shelly Radic (president, Project 1.27), in discussion with author, December 2014.

[14]Ibid.

[15]Ibid.

[16]Ibid.

[17]Ibid.

[18]Nightlight Christian Adoptions, "Snowflakes Pages," last modified December 7, 2016, https://www.nightlight.org/snowflakes-embryo-donation-adoption.

[19]Cana Brueckner (entrepreneur, Trades of Hope), in discussion with author, February 2015.

[20]Ibid.

[21]Robert Gelinas (lead pastor, Colorado Community Church), in discussion with author, January 2015.

[22]Ibid.

[23]Robert Gelinas, "Calling All Pastors," *Adopting and Fostering in Faith* (podcast), January 5, 2015, http://fosteringandadoptinginfaith.com/pastors.

Chapter Five

[1]Elizabeth Yore (international consultant in child exploitation cases, former Oprah Winfrey's Child Advocate), in discussion with author, March 2015.

[2]"Child Trafficking and Child Welfare," *Polaris*, June 2015, accessed December 23, 2016, https://polarisproject.org/resources/child-trafficking-and-child-welfare.

[3]"Sex Trafficking in the U.S.: A Closer Look at U.S. Citizen Victims," *Polaris*, May 2015, accessed December 23, 2016, https://polarisproject.org/resources/sex-trafficking-us-closer-look-us-citizen-victims.

[4]Laura Lederer, "The Health Consequences of Sex Trafficking and Their Implications for Identifying Victims in Healthcare Facilities," *Annals of Health Law* 23, no. 1 (Winter 2014), http://www.annalsofhealthlaw.com/annalsofhealthlaw/vol_23_issue_1#pg1.

[5]Ibid.

[6]"Sex Trafficking in the U.S."

[7]Ibid.

[8]Tim Hume, Lisa Cohen, and Mira Sorvino, "The Women Who Sold Their Daughters into Sex Slavery," *CNN*, 2013, http://www.cnn.com/interactive/2013/12/world/cambodia-child-sex-trade.

[9]Agape International Missions, "AIM: What We Do," http://agapewebsite.org.

[10]United Nations Office on Drugs and Crime, *Global Report on Trafficking in Persons 2014* (New York: United Nations, 2014), https://www.unodc.org/documents/data-and-analysis/glotip/GLOTIP_2014_full_report.pdf.

[11]Ibid.

[12]Brenda Zurita, "Human Trafficking Estimates and Statistics," *American Thinker*, June 10, 2014, http://www.americanthinker.com/2014/07/human_trafficking_estimates_and_statistics.html#ixzz3knh7nH84.

[13]The Associated Press, "2.4 Million Human Trafficking Victims around the World at Any Given Time: U.N.," *New York Daily News*, April 4, 2012, http://www.nydailynews.com/news/world/2-4-million-human-trafficking-victims-world-time-u-n-article-1.1055619.

[14]Genevieve Plaster, "Shock Study: 55% of Sex-Trafficking Victims Become Pregnant, Forced into Abortions," *Life News*, September 24, 2014, http://www.lifenews.com/2014/09/24/shock-study-55-of-sex-trafficking-victims-become-pregnant-forced-into-abortions.

[15]Lederer, "Health Consequences."

[16]"Child Sex Trafficking Cover Up: Planned Parenthood Covers Up Child Trafficking," *Live Action News*, http://liveaction.org/what-we-do/investigations/child-sex-trafficking-cover-up/.

[17]Kristi Burton Brown, "Forced Abortion in America: Human Trafficking Victims," *Live Action News*, September 25, 2014, http://liveactionnews.org/forced-abortion-in-america-human-trafficking-victims.

[18]Alliance Defending Freedom, "How Planned Parenthood 'Cares' for Child Victims of Sexual Abuse: A Summary of Planned Parenthood Failing to Report Sexual Abuse," September 3, 2015, http://www.adfmedia.org/files/PlannedParenthoodSexAbuseSummary.pdf.

[19] Ibid.

[20] Lederer, "Health Consequences."

[21] Steven Wagner, "Kathleen Sebelius' Gruesome Moral Calculus," *National Catholic Register*, November 29, 2011, http://www.ncregister.com/daily-news/kathleen-sebelius-gruesome-moral-calculus#ixzz2bJzTOkm3.

[22] Plaster, "Shock Study."

[23] Yore, discussion with author.

[24] Ibid.

[25] Tom Tillapaugh (president, StreetSchool Network; founder and administrator, Denver Street School System; founder, Hope Academy), in discussion with author, April 2015.

[26] Ibid.

[27] Exodus Cry, "About Exodus Cry," http://exoduscry.com/about.

[28] Blaire Pilkington Fraim (former director of intervention, Exodus Cry), in discussion with author, January 2015.

[29] Ibid.

Chapter Six

[1] Faith Fookes, "Fistula, a Silent Tragedy for Child Brides," *Girls Not Brides*, June 12, 2013, http://www.girlsnotbrides.org/fistula-a-silent-tragedy-for-child-brides.

[2] Charlotte Alfred, "How South Sudan's Conflict Is Killing Women Far from the Battlefield," *Huffington Post*, July 10, 2015, http://www.huffingtonpost.com/2015/07/10/women-in-south-sudan_n_7707560.html.

[3] "DR Congo: 48 Rapes Every Hour, US Study Finds," *BBC News*, May 12, 2011, http://www.bbc.com/news/world-africa-13367277.

[4] The Voice of Martyrs, "Egypt: Kidnapped," November 18, 2014, http://www.persecution.com/public/newsroom.aspx?story_ID=%3d373232&featuredstory_ID=%3d343636.

[5] Philip Yancey, *The Jesus I Never Knew* (Grand Rapids, MI: Zondervan, 1995), 154.

[6] Sarah Ray (executive director, Yobel International), in discussion with author, February 2015.

[7] Ibid.

[8] Kate Bryan, "New Year's Resolution: Be a One-Girl Revolution," *Catholic News Agency*, accessed March 11, 2017, http://www.catholicnewsagency.com/cw/post.php?id=693.

[9] Kate Bryan (senior account executive, CRC Public Relations), in discussion with author, February 2015.

[10] Ibid.

[11] Reggie Littlejohn (founder and president, Women's Rights Without Frontiers), in discussion with author, July 2015.

[12]Ibid.

[13]Marvin Olasky, "Complete Dependence," *World Magazine*, July 12, 2014, http://www.worldmag.com/2014/06/complete_dependence.

[14]Littlejohn, discussion with author.

[15]Ibid.

[16]Christina Bennett, "Biography," *Christina Marie Bennett: Conversations to Change a Culture* (blog), accessed March 11, 2017, http://www.chrismarie.com/bio.

[17]Christina Marie Bennett (journalist, Live Action News, Bound4Life, http://www.chrismarie.com, and more; client service manager at ABC Women's Center), in discussion with author, March 2015.

[18]Ibid.

Chapter Seven

[1]"The First 1000 Days: The Critical Start to a Child's Life," PowerPoint presentation by Becky Cash, Naturopathic Practitioner; Barbara Lagoni, Nutrition, Cornell University; and Hannah Sharapan, https://www.google.com/url?sa=t&rct=j&q=&esrc=s&source=web&cd=4&ved=0ahUKEwiB2u_n3M7SAhWHKGMKHexLDocQFggvMAM&url=http%3A%2F%2Fwww.betterfuturestartstoday.com%2Fdownloads%2Fmondaynightwebinar%2FFirst1000Days.pptx&usg=AFQjCNEimE6l-sU4eP8WCNycYPN-jMaavg.

[2]World Bank, "Poverty," http://data.worldbank.org/topic/poverty.

[3]United Nations, "World Refugee Day, June 20," http://www.un.org/en/events/refugeeday/background.shtml.

[4]Ibid.

[5]UN Refugee Agency, "Protecting Refugees & the Role of the UNHCR," 2014, http://www.unhcr.org/509a836e9.html.

[6]Ibid.

[7]Ludovica Iaccino, "World Refugee Day 2014: Living Conditions in the Largest Refugee Camps," *International Business Times*, June 20, 2014, http://www.ibtimes.co.uk/world-refugee-day-2014-living-conditions-largest-refugee-camps-1453517.

[8]UN Refugee Agency, "Protecting Refugees."

[9]Ibid.

[10]Kinship United, "Our Mission," https://kinshipunited.org/about-kinship/.

[11]Prov. 31:9.

[12]Prov. 22:22.

[13] Robert Rector, "Marriage: America's Greatest Weapon against Child Poverty," *Heritage Foundation*, September 5, 2012, http://www.heritage.org/poverty-and-inequality/report/marriage-americas-greatest-weapon-against-child-poverty.

[14]"Effects of Single Parenthood on Poverty," *Marripedia*, http://marripedia.org/effects_of_single_parents_on_poverty_rates; US Census Bureau, Current Population Survey, 2015 and 2016 Annual Social and Economic Supplements, "Table 4: Families in Poverty by Type of Family: 2014 and 2015."

[15]"Testimony of Ron Haskins, Senior Fellow, Brookings Institution and Senior Consultant, Annie E. Casey Foundation Before the Social Security and Family Policy Subcommittee of the Committee on Finance, U.S. Senate," May 5, 2004, https://www.brookings.edu/wp-content/uploads/2016/06/20040505-1.pdf.

[16]Robert Rector, "How Welfare Undermines Marriage and What to Do about It," *Heritage Foundation*, November 17, 2014, http://www.heritage.org/welfare/report/how-welfare-undermines-marriage-and-what-do-about-it. See also Rachel Sheffield and Robert Rector, "Five Myths about Welfare and Child Poverty," *Heritage Foundation*, December 20, 2016, http://www.heritage.org/welfare/report/five-myths-about-welfare-and-child-poverty.

[17]Ibid.

[18]Dave McGinn, "Couples Who Wait Report Better Sex Lives," *Globe and Mail*, last modified September 10, 2012, http://www.theglobeandmail.com/life/the-hot-button/couples-who-wait-report-better-sex-lives/article1847555.

[19]McKinley Irvine, "32 Shocking Divorce Statistics," *Family Law* (blog), October 30, 2012, http://www.mckinleyirvin.com/Family-Law-Blog/2012/October/32-Shocking-Divorce-Statistics.aspx.

[20]Tim B. Heaton, "Factors Contributing to Increasing Marital Stability in the United States," *Journal of Family Issues* 23 (2002): 392–409, see specifically 401, 407.

[21]Glenn T. Stanton, "Premarital Sex and Greater Risk of Divorce," *Focus on the Family*, http://www.focusonthefamily.com/about/focus-findings/marriage/premarital-sex-and-divorce.

[22]Tom Tillapaugh (president, StreetSchool Network; founder and administrator, Denver Street School System; founder, Hope Academy), in discussion with author, April 2015.

[23]George W. Bush, *A Charge to Keep: My Journey to the White House* (New York: Perennial, 1999), 32.

[24]Ibid., 214–17.

[25]Ibid., 217.

[26]Gene Roncone (lead pastor, Highpoint Church), in discussion with author, December 2014.

[27]Ba-Iyaka, "Animal Bank-Goat," *Partners International*, August 23, 2016, https://www.partnersintl.org/animal-bank-goat/.

[28]Jodi Visser (family friend), in discussion with author, 2014.

[29]Glenn T. Stanton, "Was the Women's March on Washington Really the Women's March?," *Glenn T. Stanton: Hope, Change, Insights* (blog), http://glenntstanton.com.

[30]Glenn T. Stanton (author, director for family formation studies at Focus on the Family), in discussion with author, December 2014.

[31]Quinn Anderson, "Our Story," *Babies of Juarez* (blog), http://babiesofjuarez.org.

[32]Quinn Anderson (founder, Babies of Juarez), in discussion with author, March 2015.

[33]Ibid.

[34]Heather Culp (missionary to Mexico and Guatemala with Casas por Cristo), in discussion with author, October 2014.

[35]Ibid.

Chapter Eight

[1]Mark Bradford, "Q&A with the Scholars: Down Syndrome and Prenatal Testing," *Charlotte Lozier Institute*, January 16, 2017, https://lozierinstitute.org/qa-with-the-scholars-down-syndrome-and-prenatal-testing/.

[2]Anne Trainer, "Abortion Is Leading Us to a 'Down's Syndrome-Free' World. I Can Barely Type the Words," *The Journal.ie*, February 4, 2017, http://www.thejournal.ie/readme/the-eighth-amendment-protected-my-son-3217231-Feb2017/.

[3]Mark Bradford, "New Study: Abortion after Prenatal Diagnosis of Down Syndrome Reduces Down Syndrome Community by Thirty Percent," *Charlotte Lozier Institute*, April 21, 2015, https://lozierinstitute.org/new-study-abortion-after-prenatal-diagnosis-of-down-syndrome-reduces-down-syndrome-community-by-thirty-percent.

[4]Ibid.

[5]Susan Donaldson James, "Prenatal Tests Have High Failure Rate, Triggering Abortion," *NBC News*, December 14, 2014, http://www.nbcnews.com/health/womens-health/prenatal-tests-have-high-failure-rate-triggering-abortions-n267301.

[6]Kristi Burton Brown, "At Eight Months, My Doctor Said He Would 'Absolutely Perform the Abortion for Me,'" *Live Action News*, March 7, 2012, http://liveactionnews.org/at-eight-months-my-doctor-said-he-would-absolutely-perform-the-abortion-for-me.

[7]"Early-Stage Embryos with Abnormalities Can Still Develop into Healthy Babies," *Wellcome Trust Sanger Institute*, March 29, 2016, http://www.sanger.ac.uk/news/view/early-stage-embryos-abnormalities-can-still-develop-healthy-babies.

[8]Kristi Burton Brown, "Scheduled by Her Boyfriend to Abort at Planned Parenthood, This Young Woman Chose Life," *Live Action News*, January 25, 2015, http://liveactionnews.org/pressured-to-abort-because-doctors-said-her-baby-would-have-deformities-this-young-woman-chose-life.

[9]Ibid.

[10] Rick and Karen Santorum, "Bella Santorum Turns Seven and Points the Way to Beauty," *National Review*, May 13, 2015, http://www.nationalreview.com/article/418302/bella-santorum-turns-seven-and-points-way-beauty-rick-santorum.

[11] Kristi Burton Brown, "TIME'S Writer Thanks Rick Santorum for His Daughter's Smile," *Live Action News*, February 27, 2012, http://liveactionnews.org/times-writer-thanks-rick-santorum-for-his-daughters-smile.

[12] Kristi Burton Brown, "Doctor Insists Parents Choose Starvation and Slow Death for Baby Born with Cleft Lip," *Live Action News*, January 31, 2013, http://liveactionnews.org/doctor-insists-parents-choose-starvation-and-slow-death-for-baby-born-with-cleft-lip.

[13] "Russia: Children with Disabilities Face Violence, Neglect," *Human Rights Watch*, September 15, 2014, http://www.hrw.org/news/2014/09/15/russia-children-disabilities-face-violence-neglect.

[14] Ibid.

[15] Will Ripley, "'They Don't Deserve This Kind of Life': Meet China's Abandoned Children," *CNN*, August 12, 2015, http://www.cnn.com/2015/08/11/asia/china-orphanage-children.

[16] Ibid.

[17] Rosa Monckton, "'The Twins I Saw Will Spend Their Lives Staring at Ceilings': Bulgaria's Abandoned Children," *Spectator*, February 9, 2013, http://www.spectator.co.uk/features/8838971/the-forgotten-ones.

[18] Adéye Salem, "My Daughter, My Story (Part One)," *Adéye Salem* (blog), March 16, 2011, http://www.nogreaterjoymom.com/2011/03/my-daughter-my-story.

[19] Adéye Salem, "Her Redemption, My New Life," *Adéye Salem* (blog), February 23, 2015, http://www.nogreaterjoymom.com/2015/02/her-redemption-my-new-life.

[20] Adéye Salem, "Life as We Both Once Knew It," *Adéye Salem* (blog), May 14, 2014, http://www.nogreaterjoymom.com/2014/05/life-as-we-both-once-knew-it.

[21] Warren Cole Smith, "*The Drop Box* Director on Coming to Christ," *World*, March 3, 2015, http://www.worldmag.com/2015/03/the_drop_box_director_on_coming_to_christ.

[22] Brian Ivie (director, *The Drop Box*; head of storytelling, Arabella Studios), in discussion with the author, March 2015.

[23] Jonathan Merritt, "This Filmmaker Set Out to Win Sundance and Got 'Saved' Instead," *Religion News Service*, February 20, 2015, http://jonathanmerritt.religionnews.com/2015/02/20/filmmaker-set-win-sundance-got-saved-instead/#sthash.DAiMoxYE.dpuf.

[24] Brian Ivie, Facebook page, https://www.facebook.com/bivie1?lst=512139333%3A730931305%3A1489384424.

[25] Ivie, discussion with author.

[26] Ibid.

[27] Kindred Image, "About Us," http://kindredimage.org/about-us.

[28] Ivie, discussion with author.

Chapter Nine

[1] Franklin Graham, Facebook status, April 9, 2015, https://www.facebook.com/FranklinGraham/posts/901018466621002?comment_tracking=%7B%22tn%22%3A%22O%22%7D.

[2] Franklin Graham, Facebook status, April 14, 2015, https://www.facebook.com/FranklinGraham?fref=nf.

[3] Alliance Defending Freedom, "Religious Freedom," http://www.adflegal.org/issues/religious-freedom/church.

[4] Michael J. Norton (founder, Colorado Freedom Institute; former senior counsel at Alliance Defending Freedom; former US attorney), in discussion with author, 2015.

[5] Ibid.

[6] Gene Roncone (lead pastor, Highpoint Church), in discussion with author, December 2014.

[7] Ibid.

[8] Greg Stier, "It's Okay to Be a Fanatic for Jesus!," *Gregstier.org* (blog), September 11, 2015, http://gregstier.dare2share.org/be-a-fanatic-for-jesus.

[9] Greg Stier (CEO and founder, Dare 2 Share Ministries), in discussion with author, February 2015.

[10] Ibid.

[11] Quin Friberg (apologist, FWC Apologetic Ministries), in discussion with author, March 2015.

[12] Seth Silvers (founding partner and CEO, Story On), in discussion with author, December 2014.

[13] Ibid.

[14] Friberg, discussion with author.

[15] Silvers, discussion with author.

[16] Friberg, discussion with author.

[17] Robert Gelinas (lead pastor, Colorado Community Church), in discussion with author, January 2015.

Chapter Ten

[1] Richard Cimino, "4 Promises of God for the Suffering Christian," *Ed Taylor* (blog), June 12, 2016, http://www.edtaylor.org/2016/06/12/4-promises-of-god-for-the-suffering-christian/.

[2] Tim Hansel, *Holy Sweat* (Waco, TX: Word, 1989), 30.

Chapter Eleven

[1] *Webster's 1828 Dictionary*, s.v. "humility," accessed March 11, 2017, http://1828.mshaffer.com/d/word/humility.

[2] David Schmidt (former managing editor, Live Action News), in discussion with the author, March 2015.

[3] Ibid.

[4] University of Colorado Denver, "Mental Health Outcomes in Children in Foster Care Improved with Mentoring, Skills Development," *Science Daily*, August 9, 2010, http://www.sciencedaily.com/releases/2010/08/100802165439.htm.

[5] CASA for Children, "April Is Child Abuse Prevention Month," accessed March 11, 2017, http://www.casaforchildren.org/site/pp.aspx?c=mtJSJ7MPIsE&b=9072145&printmode=1.

[6] Jefferson and Gilpin Country District Attorney, "First Human Trafficking Unit in Colorado DA's Office," *Jeffco.us*, accessed March 11, 2017, http://jeffco.us/district-attorney/domestic-violence-program/human-trafficking-unit/.

Chapter Twelve

[1] Original composition by the author.